The Child in the Country

COLIN WARD

The Child
in the Country

BEDFORD SQUARE PRESS

First published in 1988 by Robert Hale Limited
This paperback edition published 1990 by
BEDFORD SQUARE PRESS of the
National Council for Voluntary Organisations
26 Bedford Square, London WC1B 3HU

Set in Ehrhardt by Derek Doyle & Associates, Mold, Clwyd
Printed in Great Britain by St Edmundsbury Press Ltd,
Bury St Edmunds, Suffolk
Cover printed by Heyford Press, Wellingborough

British Library Cataloguing in Publication Data
Ward, Colin, 1924–
    The child in the country. – (Society today).
    1. Great Britain. Rural regions. Children. Social life,
    1901–
    I. Title   II. Series
    941.082088054

    ISBN 0–7199–1290–3

Contents

Foreword

When Colin Ward first told me about this sequel he was writing to *The Child in the City* he canvassed my views on what the distinctive features of a country childhood were. Without pausing to think, I launched into a stream of recollections about the Dens in which I seemed to have spent a considerable portion of my life between the ages of six and eleven. They were a bizarre assortment of tree-houses, excavations and makeshift teepees, rarely more than a few hundred yards from our homes, but we saw them as remote island refuges, where we could have a kind of tribal independence, and cook, invent, fight and tell tall stories to our hearts' content – or at least till tea-time.

Something like this is part of the experience of most country children. But, as Colin reminded me, suburban children also carve out hideaways in patches of wasteland, if they are lucky enough to find any that have not been tidied up or barricaded in. Even in the heart of cities, adventurous children nose out derelict corners to build these miniature utopias, run according to their own rules. It is part of the business of childhood, not just of the countryside.

Country children are, sadly, one of the ingredients of our nostalgia-ridden rural mythology. We still half-believe them to be blessed with special health and innocence, and to have more earth wisdom than street credibility. The reality, as Colin Ward so vividly documents here, is often that they are quite simply cut off. The factors that determine the character and quality of a country child's life are common to all children: not so much the surrounding landscape as the interior of their houses, the wealth and aspirations of their parents, the availability of education and of access to the world beyond the village.

I was fortunate in growing up in the countryside in the late 40s and early 50s, a time when social provisions for rural areas were at their zenith. There was still the framework of the old village community – work opportunities on the land, shops that delivered to every kind of house, neighbourhood pubs, village schools; yet also an extensive public transport system that provided, for teenagers especially, an escape route from suffocating rural insularity. I look back with gratitude to the way that the 'cheap evening return' ticket meant that I could spend my adolescent holidays bird-watching in the afternoons and roaming London's jazz clubs in the evening.

All that has changed, and on almost every count rural services have contracted massively. The mechanization of farming and the latest stage in a drift away from the cities that has been in progress for two centuries has turned many villages into little more than 'dormitories'. Country children of all kinds and classes are the major sufferers in this process. Those from poorer working-class families – usually the indigenous villagers, ironically – are more culturally isolated and deprived of services than children from inner city ghettoes. Yet even the better-off children suffer another kind of deprivation: sent to school in the towns and excluded from playing in the woods and fields by parents' nervousness or the fences and sprays of the new agriculture, their experiences are scarcely distinguishable from those of urban children.

But if Colin Ward's book exposes the sentimental myth of the 'country child' it also triumphantly justifies the value of a country *childhood*. Our recent history is full of examples of the growing and learning that happened when children, regardless of whether they are from a rural or urban background, live for a while in close contact with the land and other living things.

Colin Ward has, throughout his distinguished writing career, argued not just on behalf of young peoples' rights, but on behalf of the *contribution* they can make, and if *The Child in the Country* is partly a plea for a better deal for rural children, it is also an invitation to us all to learn from them. At a moment when the whole identity of the countryside is in the melting pot, that wonderfully imaginative den-making behaviour could give us more clues about the proper role of the countryside than any number of committees.

The real Story!.

Richard Mabey

Introduction and Acknowledgements

Ten years ago I wrote a book, *The Child in the City*, about the relationship between urban children and their environment. The book was, to my mind, more a celebration of resourcefulness than a catalogue of deprivations, but when it was discussed at meetings and conferences of teachers and social workers there was always somebody who would comment that, while we had a whole library of studies of the city child, rural childhood was examined only as a historical phenomenon or through rosy nostalgia.

Assumptions of city deprivation were based on an unstated comparison, it was claimed, with some ideal country environment, yet there were many country children who grew up in conditions of disadvantage and deprivation, unnoticed just because of our automatic assumptions about rural life.

I took these observations seriously but would never have been able to pursue this theme but for the award of the Susan Isaacs Research Fellowship endowed by the Memorial Fund set up by her friends to commemorate Susan Isaacs (1885-1948), the psychoanalyst who founded the Department of Child Development in the University of London Institute of Education in 1933.

I have thus every reason to be grateful for the affection that Susan Isaacs won from her colleagues and students in the academic world of child development, and to Audrey Curtis, the honorary secretary of the Susan Isaacs

Memorial Fund Trustees, and senior lecturer in Early Childhood Education in the department that Susan Isaacs founded.

For me, the most endearing thing about Susan Isaacs was the way in which she rose to the opportunities that came her way, such as the opportunity to run the Malting House School in Cambridge in the 1920s onward. An unlikely full-page advertisement in the *New Statesman* in 1924 sought an Educated Young Woman to conduct the education of a small group of children as a piece of scientific research – 'someone who has considered herself too good for teaching and who has already engaged in another occupation'. It seemed absolutely made for her, and she used this chance for close and direct observation of children's behaviour. Characteristically, she similarly seized the opportunity to serve as an 'agony aunt'. 'Ursula Wise' was the reassuring pseudonym she chose in the columns of the *Nursery World*. Nowadays, no doubt, any of us would gladly accept a commission to dispense advice in this way and to be instantly put in touch with the worries and preoccupations of readers about child-rearing, but in those days this was not one of the activities thought appropriate for academic researchers. There was a conscious effort in her work to bridge the gulf that separates the world of the professionals and the experts from that of the ordinary parent and teacher. This was epitomized in her book *The Nursery Years* which went through numerous printings after its first appearance in 1929. My copy is dated 1965, so here was a book with an unusually long life-span, particularly in a world where there are fashions in child-rearing as in everything else.

The one occasion in recent history when city and country children were brought face to face with each other, as were their teachers, was in the wartime evacuation. Susan Isaacs put together the book known as *The Cambridge Evacuation Survey*[1] and her biographer Dorothy

Gardner, praising her 'realistic common sense', remarks that, 'She did not hold a meticulously severe view of the need for rigid methods of taking evidence but said that the sincerely held opinions of teachers were well worth gathering and that even less precisely taken evidence would get them nearer the truth than anything else they could get at that stage of the problem.'[2]

I share this view. The discussion of a topic as amorphous as that of the country child, when we are by no means certain that in modern Britain such a distinctive category exists any more, rests heavily on 'the sincerely held opinions of teachers.' Notoriously teachers see only one aspect of any child's personality, but they do encounter a great many children. And since few rural teachers have spent a lifetime in rural schools, they are able, and are often very willing, to make comparisons. Susan Isaacs and her colleagues were almost unique at the time in carefully seeking and publishing the opinions of children themselves.

When I wrote about the child in the city, I became aware that in modern Britain the distinctions between city, suburb, small town and village grow less tenable as the years go by. In what sense is the country-dweller who commutes to the city, and whose children commute to the nearest urban school, to be thought of as a villager? Similarly, is the experience of the child in the Orkney Islands or on Anglesey anything like that of the child living in the green belt of a metropolitan city?

One thing that I have learned is that the children of what seem to be remote places are especially anxious to remind you that they do not spend their lives chasing sheep but follow the same fashions and play the same tapes as their urban counterparts.

Also, there is much more in common in the experiences of children in affluent families, rural or urban, than in those of rich and poor children in the same city or in the same village.

Again, I became aware when writing about city children that boys experience, explore and exploit their environment much more than girls do. This is even more true in the country. The range of activities thought appropriate for boys is far wider than for girls, who are also subject to a wider range of parental prohibitions.

The lives of rural children scarcely conform to our stereotypes. Perhaps the most ironical thing is that, among that minority of families where the breadwinners are full-time farm workers, forty per cent have incomes which fall below the supplementary benefit entitlement level. Farm workers of both sexes are the lowest-paid workers in the country. They were during the agricultural depression and they were all through the boom years of the industry, now said to be at an end.

Brian McLaughlin, in his unpublished final report to the Department of the Environment on *Deprivation in Rural Areas*, points to the implications of the fact that in Britain the poor, once the greater part of the country population, have become a minority group living amidst comparative affluence. 'As a result, many of the policies which have been devised for rural areas (e.g. transport, housing, employment etc) tend to reflect the desires and wishes of the majority, rather than the needs and aspirations of the poor.'[3] It is assumed that there are fringe benefits for the rural worker, or that living in the country is cheaper, but McLaughlin finds that over eighty per cent of poor rural workers have no fringe benefits at all and that for lack of transport poor families are dependent on those village shops that remain and are more vulnerable when they close, while, 'A common explanation given by the better-off households for not using local shops was their high costs.'

The lives of rural children are full of paradoxes and surprises for the adult observer with opinions formed by the usual preconceptions carried over from the past. But a closer look at the realities of country childhood might enable us to reduce its disadvantages and make the most of its opportunities.

I am much indebted to all those parents and teachers who have shared their recollections, experiences and impressions with me, and who have given me the opportunity to talk to children up and down the country, in and out of school. I thank the children themselves for their candour and tolerance.

I must make grateful acknowledgement to the authors and publishers of all the works quoted in the text and listed in the notes. I owe a particular debt to the work of recent researchers in this field, Adrian Bell, David Clark, Gwen Dunn, Humberside Playing Fields Association, Allan Kennedy, Brian McLaughlin, Simon Nicholson and Alan Sigsworth.

Extracts from *The Peewit's Cry – A Norfolk Childhood* by Camilla Campbell are quoted by kind permission of the author. Extracts from *The Old Century, and Seven More Years* by Siegfried Sassoon are quoted by kind permission of Messrs Faber and Faber.

It is a particular pleasure to thank Viv Arkell, John and Jean Bulman, Della Chapman, Chris Culpin, Corinne Gretton, Sue Griffiths, Keith Offord, Erica Pomerans,, Kate Riddleston, Molly and Ray Stiles, Tim and Shirley Ward.

Colin Ward

Defining the
Country Child

1 Images of Childhood

*The wild anemones in the woods in April, the last load at night of hay being
drawn down a lane as the twilight comes on, when you can scarcely
distinguish the figures of the horses as they take it home to the farm, and above
all, most subtle, most penetrating and most moving, the smell of wood smoke
coming up in an autumn evening, or the smell of the scutch fires; that wood
smoke that our ancestors, tens of thousands of years ago, must have caught on
the air when they were still nomads, and when they were still roaming the
forests and the plains of the continent of Europe. These things strike down into
the very depths of our nature ....*

*These are the things that make England, and I grieve for it that they are
not the childish inheritance of the majority of the people today in our country.*

Stanley Baldwin, *On England*, 1926

English literature abounds in the kind of autobiographical
novel in whose opening chapters our young hero (for it is
seldom a heroine) is seen in the ancient small-town
grammar school, daydreaming of the woods and fields,
while his elderly teacher is droning on about Latin
declensions. Once let out of school, his real life begins –
wandering by the river banks and up through spinney and
copse to the hilltops, observing nature with a learning eye
and absorbing the wisdom of shepherd and gamekeeper,
forester and farrier, from the lovable old poacher with a
heart of gold and from the scary old hermit whose
tumbledown cottage is really a treasure trove of country
lore and bygones.

In the urban equivalent our hero is rather lower down
the social scale. Once released from his stern mentors in
the board school, he is out and down the street like a shot,

everybody's friend in the market, besieging the old lady in the sweetshop on the corner, begging orange boxes from the greengrocer, nicking coal from the railway yard, all as a rough-and-ready apprenticeship to the life of the city.

Years later (for such stories are always set in the past) these stereotypes have become successful citizens, and when they unbend to the young graduate seeking the hand of their favourite daughter, they usually confess that, 'I was educated in the School of Life.' The point that they and their creators are making is the truism that our *real* education is gained from the physical and social environment and that 'dry-as-dust school learning', as our home-spun philosophers invariably call it, is no substitute for Life Itself.

The stereotypes are, of course, intensely literary in origin. The first owes a great deal to Wordsworth and his immense influence on the British imagination, with the long shadow of Jean-Jacques Rousseau's cult of the 'natural man' behind it, and the second belongs to a picaresque tradition stretching back through Dickens to Defoe. Teachers of English have for years sought to democratize and update these stereotypes of the separateness of urban and rural experience. Think of the whole series of excellent books with which vast numbers of children have been made familiar as they became set books for examination purposes. I am thinking of texts like Flora Thompson's evocation of Victorian rural childhood in *Lark Rise*, Alison Uttley's Edwardian *The Country Child*, Laurie Lee's idyll of the years after the First World War, *Cider With Rosie*, and Ronald Blythe's assemblage of his neighbours' recollections in *Akenfield*. Excellent books, all of them, in their examination of the relationship between children and their environment, but I often wonder if their popularity among teachers is precisely because they promote a picture of a *purified identity* of rural childhood, uncontaminated by urban influences which muddy and confuse the image.

In exactly the same way, travellers returning from Polynesia report that secondary school pupils there are obliged to read Margaret Mead's *Growing Up in New Guinea* and *Coming of Age in Samoa*, the fruit of her research in the nineteen-thirties, to learn about the world they have lost.

Moralists and educators, all through history, as Raymond Williams has entertainingly illustrated,[1] have polarized the country and the city as environments for children and have concluded that, however much the city may be a necessary provider of civilized life for sophisticated adults, nature is the only true teacher and that there is something 'authentic' or 'organic' about rural childhood. A century and a half ago the American essayist Emerson grumbled that, 'I wish to have rural strength and religion for my children and I wish city facility and polish. I find with chagrin that I cannot have both.'[2]

However, above a certain social level, parents took it for granted that their children should have both urban and rural experiences, though with a strong bias for the rural. The rich, in bringing up their children, have always been able to mingle urban and rural experiences. The possession of a town house as well as a rural estate, whether we are thinking of Imperial Rome, eighteenth-century England or nineteenth-century Russia, ensured that the children of the family gained experience of both, as well as of the drama of the transition between the two. It was expedient for the patricians that their children, or at least their sons, should gain the experience of negotiating with gamekeeper and bailiff as well as with gaming-house keeper and tailor. It was expedient that their daughters should achieve marriageability and avoid the attributes of hoydens or tomboys by being 'finished' in town before 'coming out'.

It was a matter of comfort and convenience that the gentry should desert their estates in wintertime, even if only for those little winter assembly towns where they built themselves houses for the season when the country roads were impassable. The sons and daughters rehearsed their urban roles and urban manners in these small towns. Jane Austen watched them. Least fortunate were those children of the affluent who lived at home in the country, were sent off to a boarding school also in the country, and spent their holidays in someone else's country. The ordinary urban experience passed them by, just as it passed by the children of the rural poor, until the girls were sent into service and the boys emigrated in search of work.

Not only public schools and preparatory schools but borstals, reformatories and approved schools were deliberately situated in the country, far from the temptations and stimulations of the city, for rural childhood was especially valued. 'Rousseau's Emile,' wrote Herbert Read, 'seems to have been taught in a well-furnished country house, surrounded by a well-cultivated garden with all variety of natural phenomena within easy reach. That may be the ideal environment for the unfolding sensibility of a child – personally I believe that it is.'[3]

The country may have been the ideal child-rearing environment for those who had the choice, but all through the nineteenth century the 'drift from the land' drew poor country-dwellers into the cities and the new industrial towns, out of economic necessity, in a migration as dramatic as the gigantic movements of population into the exploding cities of Africa, Asia and Latin America today. And in Britain then, just as in the Third World today, if parents were asked what they hoped to achieve by exchanging rural for urban poverty, they would reply that they had taken this decisive step for the sake of their children's future.

It is very interesting that, in the Victorian city, social problems were blamed on the 'riff-raff' of the population that was moving in from rural areas. It was thought that such areas were exporting the thriftless, unstable, footloose elements in their village population to the towns. At the very same time, observers of rural life were lamenting that the able, enterprising, stable, bright and adventurous members of the rural population were those who emigrated, leaving behind those who lacked these qualities. The diminishing rural population was thought, in the crude social Darwinism of the period, to consist of the unfit, since the movement away from rural life exemplified the survival of the fittest.

Victorian medical authorities insisted that the unhealthy cities depended on a continual migration from the country and would wither away without it. The city attracted 'the pick of the youth, both physically and intellectually', according to Dr P. Williams-Freeman, and thus encouraged 'a survival of the unfittest by elimination of the best'. For him, 'The child of the townsman is "bred too fine", it is too great an exaggeration of himself, excitable and painfully precocious in its childhood, neurotic, dyspeptic, pale, and undersized in its adult state, if it ever reaches it.'[4] For Dr J. Milner Fothergill, 'They are certainly more affluent than their country cousins; but they are town dwellers, and therefore a doomed race. Without infusions of new blood in a few generations they die out; while their country cousins remain a fertile folk.'[5]

These opinions continued to be held well into the twentieth century and were linked with the view that the country was the ideal environment for the child. When the wars in South Africa revealed the poor physical condition of recruits for the Army, a Government report concluded that, 'With a view to combatting the evils resulting from the constant influx from country to town, the Committee recommends that every effort should be made by those charged with the conduct and control of rural schools to open the minds of the children to the resources and opportunities of rural existence.'[6] And a report on delinquency underlined the Wordsworthian view that Nature was the only sound moral instructor: 'Recent developments have clearly shown that not only does juvenile delinquency increase in direct proportion to population, but it has also shown that the further a growing child is removed from the health-giving influences of the country, the more frequent are his lapses into mischief and crime. One of the most apparent effects of town life upon the character of a child is seen in a lack of reverence. Country dwellers, from an early age, are witnesses of the works of Nature, and therefore their subconscious mind is imbued with a spirit of reverence ....'[7]

Reginald Bray, a progressive member of the London County Council's education committee, found that London children lived in a disturbing atmosphere of restless excitement because, 'The concentrated power of the human element, when exerted to its full extent, creates the Hooligan; but it breeds excitement and dislike of any restraint in all alike who inhabit a large city,' just because, 'A mass of impressions are hurled at the observer, a thousand scenes sweep by him; but there is nothing to hold them together, nothing to produce a sense of order, nothing to give a perception of similarity.'[8] And the German educational philosopher Karl Weidel urged rural primary school teachers to make strenuous efforts to keep their pupils on the land: 'In contrast to the peasant, he argued, the urbanite was enamoured of intellect and skeptical of authority. He was a nomad, both physically and emotionally, and his character suffered from superficiality and inner emptiness.'[9]

But not every observer of the contrast between urban and rural childhood saw it in these terms. The nineteenth-century Russian novelist Leo Tolstoy was a sophisticated aristocrat, who yearned to be a peasant. Before he set up his village school on his estate at Yasnaya

Polyana, he gave himself a grand tour of the public education systems of Germany, France and Britain. He reached the conclusion that, 'Education is an attempt to control what goes on spontaneously in culture: it is culture under restraint.' He illustrated this from his observations in visiting Marseilles, where he went to every school attended by working people's children and had long conversations with teachers and pupils in and out of school. He witnessed mechanical rote learning of the kind taken for granted in those days, found that pupils could not read any other books than those they had studied and that, 'Six years of school had not given them the faculty of writing a word without a mistake.' He convinced himself that the schools of Marseilles were exceedingly bad.

Then Tolstoy drew a very significant conclusion: 'If, by some miracle, a person should see all these establishments, without having seen the people in the streets, in their shops, in the cafés, in their home surroundings, what opinion would he form of a nation which was educated in such a manner? He certainly would conclude that that nation was ignorant, rude, hypocritical, full of prejudices, and almost wild. But it is enough to enter into relations, and to chat with a common man in order to be convinced that the French nation is, on the contrary, almost such as it regards itself to be: intelligent, clever, affable, free from prejudices, and really civilised.'

How could this be? 'I involuntarily found an answer in Marseilles, when, after the schools, I began to stroll down the streets, to frequent the dram-shops, *cafés chantants*, museums, workshops, quays and book-stalls.'

The city, he found was itself an education: 'Whether this education is good or bad is another matter; but here it is, this unconscious education which is so much more powerful than the one by compulsion; here is the unconscious school which has undermined the compulsory school and has made its contents to dwindle down almost to nothing …. What I saw in Marseilles takes place in all the other countries: everywhere the greater part of one's education is acquired, not at school, but in life. There where life is instructive, as in London, Paris, and, in general, in all large cities, the masses are educated; there where life is not instructive, as in the country, the people are uneducated, in spite of the fact that the schools are the same in both.'[10]

Tolstoy provided an eloquent recommendation for the city as an automatic educator and, as a countryman, did not believe in Shakespeare's 'books in the running brooks, sermons in stones, and good in everything'. In fact, he reinforces a stereotype that is as old as urban life itself. The town child is knowing, quick-witted, streetwise and learns from every day's new encounters. The country child is slow, innocent and even bovine. Words like clodhopper, bumpkin, yokel and hayseed were invented to epitomize this stereotype. Like the opposite mythology, it similarly permeates literature, from the Roman Petronius to P.G. Wodehouse (who remarked that, 'About the London child there is a breezy insouciance which his country cousin lacks.') Marx and Engels, in the Communist Manifesto, wrote a famous passage about 'the idiocy of rural life' and, of course, only villages have village idiots.

2 'Village Children'

When we were nearly there we were surprised to hear the noise of boys shouting and chasing each other. Usually there was no one there except ourselves. We looked at Mother and she said, 'It is just the village boys, darlings, it's Saturday, you know. And they like playing in the woods just as much as you do, after a week of school.
Camilla Campbell, *The Peewit's Cry – A Norfolk Childhood*, 1980

When Britain entered the nineteenth century, the vast majority of its children were the children of farm labourers. By the end of that century, although Britain had become a predominantly urban nation, farm labourers were still the biggest single occupational group in the country. At that time there were two million farm workers. Today the farm labourer as such has virtually disappeared, since the 160,700 workers of 1984 were almost all skilled in handling the complex machinery of modern agriculture. (They were supplemented at certain times in the year by another 156,000 casual or part-time workers.)

Only a small minority of children living in the country today are the sons and daughters of farm workers. The 'village children' have disappeared from history. But they were scarcely ever in it, even though they were once the majority of all children. Peter Laslett, commenting on the swarms of children surrounding our ancestors, as well as on their pitifully low expectation of life, remarks that these crowds of children are strangely absent from the written record: 'There is something mysterious about the silence of all these multitudes of babies in arms, toddlers and adolescents in the statements men made at the time about their own experience.'[1]

Only our modern interest in working-class autobiography, local and oral history, has excavated the personal experiences of this silent majority of country children, buried in the bluebooks of a dozen nineteenth-century royal commissions, school logbooks and parish records, and in the handful of autobiographical writings of exceptional children of the labouring poor like the poets John Clare, born in 1793, and Robert Bloomfield, born in 1766. Village children were figures in the background of the vast literature of rural life, part of the picturesque scenery, the deserving poor who were objects of charity for the big house or the vicarage.

The perception of rural childhood that fed mythology for half a century was Mary Russell Mitford's *Our Village*, published in parts between 1824 and 1832 and continuously reprinted to this day.

Of country boys she wrote, 'In general they are an open, spirited, good-humoured race, with a proneness to embrace the pleasures and eschew the evils of their condition, a capacity for happiness quite unmatched in man, or woman, or girl. They are patient, too, and bear their fate as scapegoats (for all sins whatsoever are laid as matters of course to their door), whether at home or abroad, with amazing resignation; and, considering the many lies of which they are the objects, they tell wonderfully few in return. The worst that can be said of them is, that they seldom, when grown to man's estate, keep the promise of their boyhood ....' She does not stop to ask why, and goes on to describe Joe, a poor twelve-year-old '... as may be conjectured from the lamentable state of that patched round frock, and the ragged condition of those unpatched shoes, which would encumber, if anything could, the light feet that wear them. But why should I lament the poverty that never troubles him? ... He works at yonder farm on the top of the hill ....'

The girls, according to Miss Mitford, were 'hardier, dirtier, noisier, more sturdy defiers of heat, and cold, and wet, than boys themselves', until the age of ten, when,

> ... the little damsel gets admission to the charity school, and trips mincingly thither every morning, dressed in the old-fashioned blue gown, and white cap, and tippet, and bib and apron of that primitive institution, looking as demure as a nun, and as tidy; her thoughts fixed on button-holes and spelling-books – those ensigns of promotion .... Then at twelve the little lass comes home again, uncapped, untippeted, unschooled; brown as a berry, wild as a colt, busy as a bee – working in the fields, digging in the garden, frying rashers, boiling potatoes, shelling beans, darning stockings, nursing children, feeding pigs; – all these employments varied by occasional fits of romping and flirting, and idle play, according as the nascent coquetry, or the lurking love of sport, happens to preponderate; merry, and pretty, and good with all her little faults. It would be well if a country girl could stand at thirteen. Then she is charming. But the clock will move forward, and at fourteen she gets a service in a neighbouring town; and her next appearance is in the perfection of the butterfly state, fluttering, glittering, inconstant, vain – the gayest and gaudiest insect that ever skimmed over a village green. And this is the true progress of a rustic beauty, the average lot of our country girls; so they spring up, flourish, change, and disappear.[2]

Mary Russell Mitford's style must seem archly sentimental to people familiar with the social history of the period, but her account of the village children of Three Mile Cross, between Reading and Basingstoke, stresses truths which remained constant for a century after she wrote. The boys were destined to hard labour from childhood onward, resulting in the characteristic stooping stance and gait of Hodge, the Victorian farm worker, while the girls were equally inevitably to go into 'service' at thirteen or fourteen, first in a nearby town and then in the wider world. From childhood, they had a share of domestic tasks, and their early departure from the overcrowded cottage made more room for the younger children. Miss Mitford was a pre-Victorian and, in her account, girls under ten could behave as indecorously as the boys, something that was not considered correct in Flora Thompson's village girlhood fifty years later, when 'Victorian ideas, too, had penetrated to some extent.'[3]

And however patronizing Miss Mitford's approach, the village children were to her sentient humans rather than part of the landscape. Nothing could be more suddenly chilling than that passage in Alison Uttley's idyllic *The Country Child* when her *alter ego* Susan Garland overhears a remark as the congregation files out of the Christmas service: ' "What a very plain child that Garland child is! Positively ugly," said Mrs Drayton to her husband. Susan gasped and stood still. The world was filled with sorrow. The gleaming snow was dulled, a cloud swept over the sun, and the sky drooped. Mrs Drayton turned round and saw the girl's startled eyes. "Will you please ask your mother to send two shillings' worth of eggs?" she said stiffly, and passed on like a queen.'[4]

Or the encounter from Winifred Foley's girlhood in the inter-war years, when, 'One autumn day, I nipped down the field in the hope of finding a walnut under a tree in the corner. As I searched, a huntswoman rode up. She reined in her mount at the side of me, and in a loud, assured "county" voice, called to a male rider a few yards away: "Do come and have a look at this. Isn't it quaint?" She stared at me with such insolent amusement that I realized I was the "it" referred to ....'[5]

Although people chose to look back on village life as that of a closely knit community, it was in fact a series of quite separate communities, based on unquestioning deference. Sunday Schools began to penetrate the lives of village children from 1785, 'National' schools from 1811, and

'British' schools from 1814, and as early as 1792 William Godwin was warning that, 'Public education has always expended its energies in the support of prejudice; it teaches its pupils, not the fortitude that shall bring every proposition to the test of examination, but the art of vindicating such tenets as may chance to be established .... This feature runs through every species of public establishment; and, even in the petty institution of Sunday schools, the chief lessons that are taught are a superstitious veneration for the church of England, and to bow to every man in a handsome coat.'[6] His forecast was proved correct by every account of the schooling of the Victorian village child. Pamela Horn, in her study of their experiences, reports how,

> From time to time, too, the appearance on the road of a carriage belonging to the squire or some other village notable would jerk them back to their best behaviour. As the carriage passed it was customary for the children to draw hastily to one side and to salute the passengers in an appropriate manner. Thus at Langley Burrell in Wiltshire, Miss Constance Pearce, who was the daughter of the local brewer, remembers that at about the turn of the century, the children, who attended the village school were still 'taught to bob to the Squire's family, or Sir John Dickson's family, who lived in Pewhill house, when out on the road.' (The Squire was a Mr Ashe, and it is perhaps indicative of the awe in which he was held that, according to an earlier observer – Francis Kilvert – at the beginning of the 1870s, 'One of the Langley Burrell school children being asked, Who made the World? replied, Mr Ashe.') Similarly attitudes seem to have been displayed in a number of other parishes, and at Helmingham in Suffolk a girl who omitted on one occasion to curtsey to the Squire's lady, was apparently caned in school for this the next day.[7]

These attitudes took an immense time to die out. Stan Holmes, a farm labourer's son, now a self-employed businessman, remembers from his school days in the

1930s that, 'When the squire or farmer came along you had to stand and raise your hat to him. Same for the vicar and schoolmaster. You had to respect everybody for what they were. They had what we call a "pecking order" and you had to treat people as such. If you didn't – look out!'[8] The social distance between village children and their betters was enormous and virtually unbridgable. Thus, drawing on the recollections of two clergymen's daughters (born in 1900 and 1879 respectively), John Burnett records that, 'At higher social levels, contacts with "the poor" were deliberately avoided or carefully controlled. Margaret Cunningham, daughter of the rector of Cranleigh, was forbidden to talk to "the poor children" who attended the National (i.e. Church) School, though they offered to share a skipping rope which "I would have liked to have accepted as I was no mean skipper." Another clergyman's daughter, Ludivina Jackson, was allowed a limited contact with "the unfortunates" when she became a Sunday School teacher at the age of ten, but here the relationship was clearly one of superior and inferior, not of equals.'[9]

Village children lived in a culture of deference and dependence, and few of their 'betters' worried about their isolation from the changing outside world. The rector of Great Leighs in Essex remarked quite casually in his diary that, 'It is characteristic of the village mind that it is too feeble to accept a simple fact.'[10] In the mid-1920s J.W. Robertson Scott, founder of the magazine *The Countryman*, wrote a once-famous book, *England's Green and Pleasant Land*, about the real state of rural life behind the self-indulgent ruralism. He was bold enough to remark that, 'As one meditates on the matter one comes to see that the thing that is wrong with a large proportion of the agricultural class is something that is wrong from its childhood ...' and he declared that, 'To starve the junior schools of our hamlets is to cut at the roots of our hopes for the reformation of rural England.'[11]

A decade earlier than Robertson Scott, in 1912, the book *Change in the Village* was published. It was by George Bourne, also known as George Sturt, whose books have been known to generations of English teachers as accurate and sympathetic accounts of traditional village life and work. The author was a school teacher in rural Surrey before inheriting his family's wheelwrighting business. His book was an elegy for what he saw as a peasantry destroyed and demoralized by the enclosure of common land and by the short-lived period of 'high farming' which followed. He says, 'What was really demolished in that struggle was the country skill, the country lore, the country outlook; so that now, though we have no smashed machinery, we have a people in whom the pride of life is broken down; a shattered section of the community; a living engine whose fly-wheel of tradition is in fragments and will not revolve again.'

Bourne's final chapter, which he called 'The Forward Movement', reminded his readers that, 'Educational enthusiasts are busy; legislators have their eyes on villages; throughout the leisured classes it is habitual to look upon "the poor" as a sort of raw material, to be remodelled according to the leisured ideas of what is virtuous or refined, or useful, or nice; and nobody seems to reflect that the poor may be steadily, albeit unconsciously, moving along a course of their own ....' One agency for this change was the despised popular press, penetrating into poor rural homes. 'There is no saying,' Bourne concluded, 'what its offspring may not achieve, once they get their powers of intellect awake on modern lines and can draw freely upon the great world for ideas.'[12]

Today there are so few 'village children' in the old sense among the inhabitants of villages that we send today's children from the village to interview the old inhabitants with cassette recorders to learn what life was like in the days when the 'village community' still existed. The old people oblige, reminiscing about the way children made their own amusements, the excitement of fairs and day trips, the way their mothers struggled to maintain families on pathetically small incomes, but they also remind us of incredible hardship, squalor and exploitation well within their own memory. Sometimes they reflect upon the meaning of their own memories. Mr G.F. Seymour recalls that among the common sights of his childhood were '... children running about in all weather without boots and stockings, children in dirty ragged clothes, children who stood with their noses pressed to the panes of the baker's shop window ...', and he goes on to stress that, 'We were of course, one of the richest countries in the world. Other old people, looking back, may agree that it was a pity that those riches couldn't have been more evenly distributed .... The "good old days" are created by our memories and imaginations. The present time is really the good old days, if only people can be made to realize it, and not blind themselves to the facts of how tough life can be ....'[13]

3   Global Villagers

Urban and metropolitan values and norms dominate English society, and whether people actually live in country villages or in the city, they are the products of a broadly similar educational system; they dress alike; they read the same newspapers and watch the same television programmes. In brief, unlike many other countries of the world, it is increasingly difficult in England to speak of a rural culture which is distinctive in significant ways from the mainstream urban and metropolitan culture of our society. Nevertheless, there lingers in many rural areas a constellation of values, dispositions, and understandings and modes of thought, reinforced in every succeeding generation, which may be regarded as characteristically rural and are the remnant of the old rural culture (sometimes called the 'prior' or 'residual' culture) which, in many areas, has been almost totally eclipsed.

Anthony Russell, *The Country Parish*, 1986

The sludge-gulper paid its yearly call unexpectedly. It is a converted tanker with yards of expensive flexible pipe that tours our part of the county emptying cesspools.

'Look,' I said to two visiting eight-year-olds whose family has lived round here for generations, 'Santa Claus is early this year.'

Old Mr Green instantly fell into the role. 'What do you want me to bring you then?' he asked.

'A computer,' said one.

'A video,' said the other.

'I'll see what I can do,' he replied, 'but I was going to bring *you* a sledge, and *you*,' pointing an admonitory finger, 'a beautiful white rabbit in a hutch.'

Like the rest of us, he has a generational view of village childhood and of village life. He remembers how foresight, improvisation, skill and hours of spare-time labour used to be a substitute for purchasing-power in providing for children's needs and yearnings. Given half a chance, he, like everyone of any generation, will look back on the days when the village was self-sustaining and made its own amusements.

We all have, according to temperament, two contrasting perceptions of the village.

One is of the ancient, unchanging community, somehow insulated from time, meeting most of its needs from its internal economy, with its blacksmith and farrier, carpenter, builder and undertaker, general store and carrier (maintaining a few, if regrettable, contacts with the outside world), and its life centred around the pub and the church, with its rectory whence the rector's wife and daughters dispensed charity to the deserving poor.

The other perception of the village is of the contemporary village, inhabited by commuters, week-enders and the retired, with the indigenous population confined to the estate on the fringe, where the smithy is now a petrol station, the pub is full of fake beams and pool tables, while of the two general stores one is an antique shop and the other a wine bar and restaurant.

A whole shelf of books describes the transition from one of these perceptions to the other, dating the change from the time when the authors ceased to be children. Thus, 'During the 1940s the scene was virtually as it had been for generations, apart from one or two mechanical innova-tions, with men working on the land, boys following in their fathers' footsteps, and women busying themselves with the home and family. Characters who had been moulded by the hardness of life, the machinations of moneymaking, or the infidelity of the elements, lived and worked together in the village to form a real com-munity ....' But there has been 'a change from a simple and palpable past to an ephemeral present and an impersonal synthetic future' because, 'Children now learn about sex from school manuals, men and women commute daily into towns for employment, the seasons of the year are unimportant ....'[1]

People have made similar observations throughout history, as Raymond Williams shows,[2] but a whole series of important points needs to be made about the view of history this represents.

The first is that far more devastating changes occurred in rural life at the time when landowners pursued their policy of enclosure;[3] the second is that the whole thrust of the agricultural industry for 150 years has been to dispense with labour, and that the days when it was possible for us to see 'boys following in their fathers' footsteps' ended long before the author I have quoted was born, while the days when girls wanted to follow in their mothers' footsteps, not into domesticity but into domestic service, ended when they realized that there were alternatives to the exploitation involved. A new generation of domestic employers brings into English rural life servants from the poor half of the world, sending their International Postal Orders back home from the village post office just to support their families. There are villages where the crucial decision about whether a sub-post office remains viable depends on such global accidents.

The third point to be made is that villages were never hermetic communities: there always were comings and goings; and the fourth is that rural settlements have always consisted of several different communities who happened to occupy the same territorial space. The gap between them in the past was infinitely greater than the gap between different rural residents today. The class gradations of English society (and to an even greater degree in the Anglo-ascendency in Wales, Scotland and Ireland) ensured that village people and village children lived in a world entirely different from that of their betters.

The fifth point that has to be stressed is that for the same century and a half in which poor people have been obliged to leave the village in the hope of actually earning a living, those with more freedom of choice moved in. When Howard Newby, a leading rural sociologist, wrote of 'the invasion of rural villages by a largely alien, urban, immigrant middle class',[4] he was simply echoing the worries expressed sixty-five years ago by a chronicler of the decline of the village community, who noted how, 'The advent into many villages of families from outside, usually of the professional or business classes, which we have seen as beginning during the close of the nineteenth century, has had some effect on the social life of the areas into which they have come ... they frequently set about organising amusements in the villages in which they have settled.'[5] But a century earlier Cobbett was complaining of '... a gentry, only now-and-then residing at all, having no relish for country delights, foreign in their manners, distant and haughty in their behaviour, looking to the soil only for their rents ... unacquainted with its cultivators, despising them and their pursuits'.[6]

The final and most important point that has to be made about change in the village, however it is regarded, is that it has at last ended the isolation of the country child. The traditional role of the country girl, if she dared look beyond domestic labour, has been immortalized explicitly in Mozart's operas *The Marriage of Figaro* and *Don Giovanni*, reinforced by a dozen homespun dramas from *Maria Marten* to *She Was Poor But She Was Honest*. The traditional role of the country boy was one of endless toil, followed by destitution when he was past it. If he escaped from this into domestic service, he was already at a disadvantage because of his red face and knobbly hands and because, even in childhood, he had acquired the stooping gait of the agricultural worker, accustomed to heavy loads too soon, and did not fit well into a footman's uniform.

This is why the steady advance of mass communications

into rural society has been a blessing and, quite simply, a *liberation* for rural children, providing just a glimpse of the outside world which was always taken for granted by their social superiors. It has been an accelerating process, often deplored and seldom celebrated. For example, a book was published in 1985 called *When Telephones Reach the Village*.[7] It was, of course, about the developing world. The only discussion of the impact of the telephone on British rural life that I have come across was, significantly, in the recollections of a country doctor, describing his life and work in the inter-war years in Dunmow, Essex, and the pathetic poverty of many of his patients.[8]

The first of these liberating lifelines to the wider world was the network of railway branch lines opened in the mid-nineteenth century, linking remote rural settlements with metropolitan life and culture. The railway station was

... the place where news came from the outside world either by telegraph – provided on the railways long before post offices began transmitting telegrams – or by newspaper or word of mouth. It was the place where every piece of invention of the Victorian age could first be seen – from the railway's own telegraph instrument and signalling system, newest engine or crane, the threshing machines, mangles, toilet cisterns and bicycles. And here troops would arrive to quell local disturbances or uprisings, and whence local organisers of the Anti-Corn-Law League and early unions went off to national gatherings. Just how important the station was to the life of the community can be gauged from the numerous stretches of approach road and land that were improved at the ratepayers' expense, widened and often given pavements which look particularly incongruous leading from nowhere today, and lit with gas lamps. In many cases the gas came from new works with their own coal sidings beside the station.[9]

Even the standardization of Britain's clocks did not come until it was enforced by railway timetables. The railway brought and stocked the village shop, and the station tavern was an alternative to the backroom alehouse. It also offered access to new markets and alternative sources of employment with wages which, however low, were higher than those prevailing in agriculture. It made commuting possible and thus caused more village residents to have livelihoods which did not depend on traditional rural occupations.

At one social level the railway meant for children the termly journey to and from boarding schools, at another the daily journey to the grammar school in the nearest market town, but for all children the sights, sounds and smells of the railway became a pervasive reminder of other places and of adventures, escape and excitement. But the great age of the train coincided with the agricultural depression that began in the 1870s and continued, with a brief respite in the First World War, until 1939. An endless stream of boys and girls, at an age when today they would be in the early years of secondary education, were brought by the carter or carrier to the railway station with their tin trunks or home-made wooden cases to depart to earn the income that rural employment could no longer provide.

The railway brought with it the cheap, popular press, which, as we have seen, was thought by George Bourne to be a powerful vehicle for change: 'It resembles that which, in a smaller way, springs from the opportunities of travelling afforded by railways. Just as few of our people now are wholly restricted in their ideas of the world to this valley and the horizons visible from its sides, but the most of them, in excursion holidays at least, have seen a little of the extent and variety of England, so, thanks to the cheap press, ideas and information about the whole world are finding their way into the cottages of the valley; and at the present stage it is not greatly important that the information is less trustworthy than it might be. The main thing is that the village mind should stretch itself, and look beyond the village; and this is certainly happening.'[10]

The bicycle brought personal mobility even to children, and the mere mention of this revolution to really old people brings a flood of recollections of the way in which they or their fathers cobbled together from abandoned old bikes and spare parts a machine which would actually work. 'When I think of the miles I covered on that rickety old bone-shaker, I can't believe it myself.' The charabanc and the bus filled in the gaps in the rail network, competed with it and, of course, eventually supplanted it, though very inadequately.

But the bus too had its rural heyday. Its historian, John Hibbs, who was once a Suffolk bus proprietor and is now director of Transport Studies at Birmingham Polytechnic, claims that the country bus belonged to country people to an extent that was never true of the railway, since the crews and the travellers knew each other intimately and there was no 'superior officer up the line'.[11] Services would accommodate the children's Saturday morning visit to 'the pictures' in town, as well as their elders' late-evening cinema trip, the Sunday School outing as well as the darts team's pub crawl. Our local paper recalls this close relationship: 'A shopping basket on a pillar box indicated one passenger was expected to be picked up. The back two pairs of seats on the village market bus from Orford to Ipswich had to be removed to cope with the passengers' purchases from the Tuesday market. Several boxes of cabbages, some dead rabbits and a live goat were carried on the outward journey. The return carried groceries, seed potatoes, perhaps a roll of new linoleum, a new spade, batteries for the wireless and rolls of wire netting which would go on the roof-top luggage rack.'[12] Small children could travel unaccompanied, for they were surrounded by friends.

The peak of accessibility for village and hamlet was

reached by the 1950s, when both rail and road services existed on a scale which, in the 1980s, seems like that of an impossible golden age. Railway enthusiasts write bitterly that, 'The massacre of country stations which accompanied the dismemberment of the British rail network in the 1960s permanently diminished the lives of the villages these stations had served. Nothing equivalent took their place. 'The bus services which replaced the train service did not long survive. Instead the planners condemned many villages to long, slow, lingering decline. Like so many of the decisions of sixties planners, this cruel decision has brought both spiritual and physical desolation in its wake.'[13] The reason why this seems an exaggeration is, of course, the immense growth in private motoring. 'The growth of mass car ownership has been a major factor in reducing the need for rural buses, and between 1951 and 1977 the number of passenger miles travelled by car increased from 40 million to 240 million. From 1965 to 1975, the number of passengers carried by country buses fell by approximately 30 per cent .... While, in major urban areas, 25 per cent of all travel is currently by public transport and 66 per cent by car, in rural areas only 14 per cent is by public transport and 81 per cent by car.'[14] Poor rural families have to make painful sacrifices in other areas of their budget to run a car. 'One respondent remarked "What man in his right mind would try to run a car on my wage? But living here, ten miles from the nearest town, I have no choice." Another man, whose wife was a diabetic in need of frequent medical treatment, explained: 'I have to keep a gallon of petrol in the car for emergencies. We never use the car for pleasure, just for essential shopping trips or trips to the doctor. If we forget anything it's just too bad. We can't afford another journey[15].' Malcolm Moseley stresses that, 'All the evidence points to the liberating effect of car availability', but that, even in a car-owning household, the car used by one adult for work is not available to anyone else, that only sixty-four per cent of men and twenty-one per cent of women hold a driving licence and that this percentage is far smaller among people over sixty-five and those in unskilled and skilled manual occupations. And, of course, twenty-six per cent of the population is too young to hold a driving licence. 'Collectively these people comprise the *majority* of the rural population. The view that the rural accessibility problem affects only a "residual minority" is a myth.'[16]

The aspect of the revolution in communications that has made 'global villagers' of all of us is, of course, the advent first of radio and then television. They profoundly affect the lives of children, and of everyone else. Moralists, psychologists and sociologists debate their influence. Howard Newby believes that, 'What the farm worker observes on his television set are the often distant and somewhat alien mores of the urban, industrial world. He may regard them as curious examples of another civilization or occasionally view with incredulity the ways of city people and industrial workers, but he will only regard them with envy when television reinforces the evaluations already implanted personally by friends and kin with whom he identifies. Otherwise television merely reinforces a point of view already strong among farm workers – that there is a wide and unbridgeable gulf between people who live in the countryside and those who live in towns.'[17] Others deplore the impact of television, using the same kind of language that was used in the 1920s and 30s about the weekly visit to the cinema: that it implants into the hitherto 'unspoiled' rural young a spurious, synthetic and second-hand veneer of sophistication. What it undoubtedly does is ensure that, in town and country alike, children are exposed to the same images and influences, are familiar with the same sights and sounds. Kenneth Fox, attempting to look back from the standpoint of a century hence, concluded that, 'Television alleviated some drawbacks of isolated family life .... It was a minimally adequate substitute for activities that were convenient and inexpensive in a dense city community, but became time-consuming and costly elsewhere .... Whether substituting TV for live entertainment and community events degraded the quality of cultural life was a question debated at great length ... [but] television provided families with a sense of participation in a common national culture.'[18]

Those who most deplore the globalization of life are invariably people who take for granted their own access to a wider culture than that of the traditional village, and they also deplore the fact that the advent of television has the corollary that today's rural children spend far less of their time in active recreation or exploration of their locality. The television correspondent of the *East Anglian Daily Times* reports that among children in the region between eight and fourteen 'Favourite activities were cricket and football for 29 per cent of boys, and swimming for 15 per cent of girls, against six per cent and two per cent respectively who enjoyed televison most' but that watching television took up most of the free time of thirty per cent of boys and forty-five per cent of girls. In the fifteen to nineteen age range, 'Although only two per cent of boys prefer watching television to anything else, 24 per cent of them spent most of their free time in front of the box. With girls 36 per cent spent most of their spare time viewing, although only nine per cent enjoyed it most.'[19]

The sociologist Denis Pym, who lives in Polstead, Suffolk, told me that, 'The cut-off point is thirty-five. People round here above that age know every field and hedge. They are familiar with every inch of the landscape. Below that age, apart from the handful who earn their living on it, they know very little.' And the naturalist Richard Mabey says regretfully, 'When I was a child, twenty-five years ago, I can remember the woods and fields brimming with other children, climbing trees, building camps, cooking, trading, tramping about the footpaths in little packs reciting rude limericks, and disappearing into the bushes for private experiments. The older ones would sometimes wander off in pairs, and we would catch enthralling, ethereal glimpses of them in pink tangles under the hedges, or glowing palely under the moon in harvest fields. Now the only loving couples you see are wedged into the back seats of parked cars.'[20] He attributes this emptying of the landscape not to the seductive influence of television but to the determination of farmers and landowners to keep people off their land.

Similarly Gwen Dunn, a Suffolk village school head teacher who had the rare opportunity to make a meticulous study of the impact of television on the lives of young children, remarks that, 'We sometimes think that children have changed because adult habits have changed.'[21] Teachers would say to her that, 'Children who have friends knocking on the door, and outings, will still relinquish television for other things. Where there are no other things, they'll just go on watching.' She comments gently that what happens with regard to friends knocking on the door depends on how many doors are opened for children.

The Urban-Rural Divide

4   The Impossible Experiment

I don't know whether you'll like me saying this, but we always had snotty noses, and then when we were evacuated into the country we discovered that your nose didn't have to be running all the time – you could breathe, you see. We realized that we'd been living in absolute muck. We did see a different sort of life when we were evacuated.

Mary Sweeney, *My Life Till Now*, BBC Radio 4, 2 April 1986

There are several enormously interesting social experiments that, happily, cannot be conducted. The first is that of allowing a child to rear itself devoid of parentage, in the wild. Truffaut's film *L'Enfant Sauvage* told the true story of Dr Itard's attempt to tame the wild boy of Aveyron, but the sad truth is that there are now no feral children, only feral parents.[1]

The second forbidden experiment is that of dropping a group of children on a deserted island just to see how they manage. This whole area of speculation has been pre-empted from discussion by William Golding's novel *Lord of the Flies*. It instantly gained the status of an O-level text and is used in schools in over forty countries. Its author was awarded the Nobel Prize for Literature. The late A.S. Neill was almost alone in commenting that, while the book would be read by thousands and the film seen by millions, not many would question its message. 'I fear that too few will ask whether boys on a desert island really would become savages and sadists; few will wonder how Golding can know how boys would behave. Naturally he doesn't, any more than you or I know.'[2]

There actually is an account of a real-life situation like this, told by Susanna Agnelli in a book about something quite different, but we are seldom anxious to learn that real life is not the same as our preconceptions:

> In 1977, six boys in Tonga, all friends, went fishing. Their boat was caught in a storm and after several terrifying days was wrecked on a reef. The crew had just enough strength to scramble ashore, onto an unknown tropical island. They realized that it was totally uninhabited. Confronted with their predicament, they promised each other that as long as they were there they would never quarrel, because that would spell the end of them; that they would always go about in pairs, in case one had an accident or got lost; and that two of them would keep guard, day and night. They kept their promises, and fifteen months later were found and rescued. They owed their survival to a shared faith; to the fact that none had any reason to exploit the other; and, especially perhaps, to a culture which gave more weight to co-operation than to competition.[3]

The third impossible experiment really happened too. What would you learn if you dropped a huge sample of city-bred children in a rural environment? It actually happened in 1939, when thousands of city children were evacuated to the country while Britain was trembling under threat of aerial bombing. After the first batch of children trickled home when the anticipated bombing failed to ensue, it happened again after the terrible Blitzkrieg summer of 1940, and yet again in the final year of the war.

Psychologists and sociologists realized that something unique was going on before their eyes. Between 1 and 4 September 1939, 1½ million people left British cities for unknown rural destinations. They were mostly unaccompanied children, and their adventures were closely observed.

If we look from the standpoint of the late twentieth century, thinking about whether such an exercise in mass migration could be performed today, the most interesting thing of all is that it was conducted by voluntary labour. Urban teachers had experienced a rehearsal a year before and in 1939 found themselves becoming substitute parents, diplomats and youth club organizers, while waiting for their pay to come through, since they often had to maintain two households and were desperately trying to keep in contact with their own children somewhere else. Their only reward was that they became a lifeline for their pupils as the one contact with everything that was familiar and re-assuring. Rural receivers, like the 17,000 members of the Women's Voluntary Services who assembled to distribute the evacuees, were unpaid, obviously.

Beyond the record of muddle and confusion that accompanied the whole evacuation exercise, the modern reader responds with either incredulity or disapproval to the idea that a rural railway signalman, faced with an unexpected volume of emergency traffic, could shunt a trainload of children to this or that location at the pull of a lever and that this instant but responsible decision could affect the lives of hundreds. Could we manage better today?

The immediate effect of evacuation was the revelation of the fact that one nation contained not one or two but half a dozen different ways of living, graduated according to income and opportunity: 'Although some effort was made to match billets and evacuees, some slum children found themselves in stately homes cared for by grumbling servants, while "respectable" mothers and children might find themselves sharing a lowly cottage, daunted by earth closets, oil lamps and water pumps. Long-standing class rituals were under strain – what time to have supper, whether to eat together or not, what to eat, whether to wear best clothes on Sunday or to work, how often to bath and the difficulty of sharing rations were issues that quickly led to considerable tensions.'[4] This is a mild but accurate description of what happened in the impossible experiment.

The worthy people in charge of billeting found themselves in charge of a host of children who, in their view, normally lived on bread and jam or fish and chips, slept under the bed, rather than in it, peed in the corner of the room and were foul-mouthed, dirty and verminous.

Malevolent rumours and horror stories spread like wildfire, improved with each re-telling, but unlike some wartime tales, they had a foundation in fact. There were two ways of responding to them. The phrase 'problem families' was invented to describe those feckless urban parents who so neglected their children.[5] But if whole populations were guilty of these shortcomings, the issue was one of problem societies rather than of inadequate individuals. The people who had been trying to draw attention to the effects of poverty, inadequate housing and poor diet all through the 1930s, suddenly found that they had an audience. The Women's Group on Public Welfare found that its report *Our Towns, A Close-Up* became a best-seller, reprinted three times in one year. Today we would not accept its moralizing language, but it concluded that 'Great and radical reforms are needed to give humanity a chance'.[6]

Even the Prime Minister was affected by the incidental revelations of evacuation: 'Neville Chamberlain, who had been a leading figure in the pre-war National Government's denial of the problem of child malnutrition, was so shocked by the stories of the children's condition that he commented to his sister, "I never knew that such conditions existed, and I feel ashamed of having been so ignorant of my neighbours. For the rest of my life I mean to try and make amends by helping such people to live cleaner and healthier lives".'[7]

There was at the same time a whole series of studies at a psychological level of the trauma of evacuation. Dorothy

Burlingham and Anna Freud produced their report on *Young Children in War-time*,[8] while Susan Isaacs and her colleagues collected the *Cambridge Evacuation Survey* which carefully sought the views of children themselves and those of their teachers.[9] A similar survey was conducted from Oxford.[10] The social investigators revealed whole levels of child life that were invisible to the social moralists. No shaper of post-war policy, for example, could have taken into account that one of the keenly felt deprivations of wartime children was the separation from domestic pets – cats, dogs or birds – or that personal *freedom* was one of the things they valued most:

Boy 15: The first thing I miss is the freedom, we are not allowed to do just as we would if we were at home.

Girl 13: I miss the freedom I had when I was at home, and the liberty of the house ....

Boy 14: I also miss the freedom of my own house.[11]

Girl 13: I cannot do as I like in the house. I must also come in when I am told and sit down and eat my meals properly and not run out into the streets with a slice of bread in my hand.[12]

These recognizable reactions are far from the standard contemporary picture, and John Macnicol comments that, 'Evacuation, in fact, revealed the essential solidarity of working-class family life – quite the opposite of what many middle-class observers maintained. The most common reason for children returning to the danger areas was homesickness for parents and relatives, or parents worrying endlessly about them.'[13]

Historians of social welfare show that the impossible experiment of evacuation was a powerful force in shaping the post-war welfare state, just because of its revelations. Richard Titmuss argued this eloquently, and Arthur Marwick remarks that, 'Ultimately the significance of the evacuation experience was that it brought to middle- and upper-class households a consciousness for the first time of the deplorable conditions endemic in the rookeries and warrens which still existed in Britain's great industrial cities, and so, among the articulate few, aroused a new sense of social concern.'[14]

I have never come across a rural child's account of the impact of evacuation, though I have met people who recalled an unexpected liberation from the fact that the frequent 'doubling-up' arrangement in village schools meant that they used the school in the mornings while the evacuated school used it in the afternoons. This enabled them to work in the afternoons as agriculture suddenly became important once more for the nation's survival.[15] Some evacuee children were pitchforked into the same situation: 'Billeting allocation was frequently chaotic: host families could be hostile; children might be selected according to their good looks and manners; in rural areas, farmers often gleefully snapped up the strongest boys and set them to work on the land.'[16] The typical farmer in 1939 was as poor as his employees, and it was considered a triumph in that year when the farm workers' minimum wage was fixed at £2.10s. In such households the billeting allowance (10s. 6d. for the first child and 8s a week for each subsequent child) was an immense increase in the family income. The grumbles about its inadequacy came from people who were not employed in agriculture and who had no idea how their neighbours lived, let alone how the urban poor survived.

One evacuee whose life was changed by this chance encounter, Martin Davis, told me of his introduction to rural life: 'I was eleven, and after our bread-and-cheese supper, I was sent to bed, with a candle, with my foster-parents' son Dick. I put on my pyjamas, he slept in his underclothes, an antiquated garment called combinations. He was up at dawn to feed the pigs and collect the eggs, and I soon followed him. I tried to emulate him in every way, eating all the stews and dumplings, sleeping in my Aertex pants and vest, chopping wood and spitting on the brussel sprouts as we picked them on a freezing morning. Dick's Mum was mortified. "Whatever would your mother say?" she remonstrated.'

But there was often trouble when the evacuee children and country children mixed. In 1985 a local historian in Glemsford, Suffolk, after immense correspondence, organized a reunion of evacuees and local children. About 120 people attended the fortieth anniversary get-together. 'It gives people a chance to thank them for what they did,' said one visitor, remembering her hosts, but another '... pointed to the school playground where he remembered being the victim of a group of children who all wanted to fight him because he was the first evacuee'.[17] Susan Isaacs reported at the time that, 'It is certain that evacuees and local children in the same playground have not mixed. Towards the end of the first year of evacuation a natural convergence of interests seems to be appearing, and a mutual understanding is beginning to emerge, but the process has been slow.'[18]

There were some children to whom rural life was the revelation for which, it seemed to them, they had always been waiting: 'To this day, the mid-1980s, the effects of rural-urban interactions as a result of war-time evacuation are still apparent. For example, many evacuees after the war stayed on in the villages to which they had been assigned, intruding upon the locals with their outlandish ways and accents, waiting sometimes for years to gain village approval.'[19]

Evacuation to the country was a shaping influence in many lives. The geographer Keith Wheeler told me how, when he was a Wandsworth boy of eleven, the secondary school he was about to join was evacuated to Hampshire, where, unlike most evacuees, he stayed all through the war years. So he grew up not on south London commons but in 'deep rural surroundings framed by intimate, detailed landscape variations over chalk, sand and clay, richly treed, and unchanged for the most part since Victorian times'. It was natural for him, as it was for his hosts, to cultivate an allotment 'in an area of deep brown loamy soil, like a rich cake, which yielded crops with little cultivation' on which he grew potatoes and giant sunflowers.

The most absorbing tale of the conversion of a town boy into a country child comes from Alex Hastie, who was six years old when he was evacuated from North Shields, remembering the potato pit, the pig-killing and the bottling of eggs, and the routine of ferreting for rabbits, gutting them and preparing them for the pot or the market. Mr Hastie spent only two years as an evacuee, but the experience has shaped his whole life:

The 1941 winter was very bad; we were unable to attend school for six weeks because of the snow. At one time it totally covered the cottage. Work was restricted to the farmyard, the animals having been brought in before the snow fell. Winter entertainment was considerable; the Wilsons were into country dance music. The two eldest lads played accordions, Tom the drums. Many a good night was had with their friends, Mrs Wilson providing the food and all playing till the early hours. It was winter when we had ice-cream. Ice was taken off the rain-barrels, crushed and mixed with milk, sugar, cornflour, served on dishes in front of the fire. The big event of the week was meeting the weekly bus. It arrived every Saturday at nine a.m. en route for Rothbury. When it returned at eight, the locals met it; long discussions were had with the passengers, relaying news of the area. I often wondered what time the driver finished. It was also a parcel-delivery service. We walked to school each day, taking sandwiches for lunch. Miss Black taught five-year-olds to fourteen-year-olds, all in the same room. In winter it was heated by a pot-bellied stove in the front. The evacuees sat at the back, far away from it. My mother sent me a corduroy jacket to wear. It had a strong smell and Miss Black made me hang it outside to get rid of the smell. I protested bitterly because of the cold, but it fell on deaf ears. I put up with this a few days, then decided to give up school. I used to go up into the fields, passing the time with the ploughmen. Eventually Mrs Wilson found out. First her lads tried to take me to school, but I escaped. Then Mrs Wilson tried, with the same results. The final result was a letter home, and the end of evacuation, aged eight. Living at Scrainwood gave me a love of country life which has had a profound influence ever since.[20]

Nothing could possibly be added to this marvellous account of life as an evacuee who was an instinctive country boy, except the point that, just as the impossible experiment of evacuation revealed the neglect of the poor in the cities, so it revealed the extent to which such automatic urban amenities as sewerage, water mains, gas and electricity were absent from the country, and that health services were minimal.

The long-suffering city teachers found that rural schools were lacking in the most basic of educational amenities. They commented on an incredible gap that remained long after evacuation was just a memory: 'When I first became headmistress of one of the 3,000 small rural schools the Plowden Report (of 1967) describes, the children and I shared the same bucket lavatory, there was no hot water, a mud patch with an unfenced pond to one side of it was the playground, a leaking oil cooker stood in the larger classroom, approximately 450 square feet lit by two sixty-watt bulbs. Not long before, that room had been the day-time lodging of sixty children between seven and fourteen years old. All this in the second half of the twentieth century: there is nothing new about adults knowingly depriving children. Excuses for doing so change according to period and fashion.'[21]

The evacuation of children was one of those factors in the Second World War that brought an immense new range of experiences to the British people, by no means as devastating as those of the other nations of Europe but profound in their effects. John Macnicol finds a significant illustration of this in the personal disruption of individual lives: 'In 1939 less than half the population left home even for a single night of the year; yet during the course of the war there were 60 million changes of address in a civilian population of 38 million.'[22]

The end of the war swept in Clement Attlee's Labour Government with a programme of reform aiming at the universal provision of public services: education, health, housing and social welfare, on a scale wider than any political programme before or since. These included, with all-party consent, comprehensive planning legislation, the protection of agricultural land, and a determination that the farming industry should not slip back into its pre-war neglect. The inherent differences in welfare and opportunity between town and country were destined to disappear.

One of the many accounts of evacuation concludes that, 'Their experiences helped the young evacuees to become libertarian, at least in the sense that they often became acutely aware of the social and economic differences that prevailed in pre-war Britain. One person remarked, significantly, that the evacuees "will return home having enjoyed the freedom and beauty of the countryside, to the drab London streets. Having tasted of the fruits of such a good life, they will be very loath to settle down once again to the old routine of home." They knew their homes better after evacuation than before. As a result, they demanded change, and frequently they got it.'[23]

This was one of the unexpected results of the impossible experiment.

5   Odious Comparisons

And then the country children, with their heavy boots and woollen stockings, coat pockets stuffed with stones and conkers, and occasionally the odd grass-snake or mouse. There were pinched, as well as rosy faces. Until they got to know you, the children had little to say for themselves. They were not very used to visitors. But, under benevolent pressure they would, in the end, tell me something about themselves, their hobbies and their homes. There were still those who were finding difficulty with reading and writing at the age of twelve and thirteen. And charming dullards (though not in the fields) who had still not mastered the intricacies of long division, and who would be leaving the term after next to work on the farms. Yet the heart of these country schools was generally sound. When they were good they were very good indeed. When they were bad, they were horrid.

Leonard Clark, *The Inspector Remembers,*
Diary of an HMI 1936–1970, 1976

School inspectors depend on experience, intuition and impressions, just like the rest of us. One of them told me that he had six infallible tell-tale signs by which to assess both a school and a teacher – but he declined to disclose them. Henry Morris, the celebrated Director of Education for rural Cambridgeshire, would visit schools unannounced to check whether there were flowers on the windowsills, and would fly into a temper if they were in a jamjar and not in a vase or pot.

The Department of Education and Science has for years been earning the hostility of teachers through its rhetoric about the 'assessment of performance'. Whose performance is really being assessed – that of the institution, that of individual teachers or that of the particular sample of conscripted children on the school roll? This is not a random sample, for it depends on the catchment area, which in turn affects the likelihood of a certain parental background, occupation and income, as well as on the availability of alternatives.

At first sight it would seem simple to apply a battery of tests or statistical surveys to get beyond anecdotes and subjective impressions to assess the relative intelligence, educational attainments, social competence, career prospects, health and happiness of urban and rural children. In practice, although differences by region or by county in many factors affecting children are well established and documented,[1] attempts to make valid urban and rural comparisons are beset with a range of difficulties, first of definition and then of interpretation. It used to be taken for granted that rural children were automatically healthier than their urban counterparts, just as we assume today that there is greater access to health services for the urban child, but these assumptions, both now and in the past, relate to social class rather than physical environment.

In countries with huge land areas, such as the United States and the Soviet Union, and in countries where there are modern sophisticated cities but a primitive 'undeveloped' hinterland, such as many in Latin America, Africa or Asia, standard educational tests can provide a clear measurement of differences between urban and rural children, once researchers become aware of the pitfalls of cultural differences which may give an automatic advantage to one group over another, since the method of testing may favour one particular form of 'intelligence' or of childhood experience or may disadvantage children belonging to a culture in which problem-solving is normally a collective rather than an individual activity. Although Britain has a common educational culture, it has no agreed measure, beyond common sense, to define the rural child – and certainly no standard definition of 'rural':

'Some social geographers have developed indices of rurality, and planners and administrators (since the demise of the rural district council) have found it necessary to devise arbitrary delineations between urban and rural areas .... The Scott Committee on Land Utilization in Rural Areas (1942) suggested that any compacted grouping of over 1,500 people was a town. At about the same time, Professor Dudley Stamp suggested that 500 was about the minimum size for a village. More recently, R.J. Green has suggested that a population of 5,000 marks the watershed between rural and urban.'[2]

Even if we accept a combination of these or other available definitions, problems remain. Is the commuting schoolchild of commuting parents who happen to live in a rural area a country child? American sociologists, faced with the existence of a 'gradient' of urban influences on the rural population, have developed a formula which suggests that, 'The extent of urban influence in the outlying hinterland varies inversely with the distance to the nearest city, and directly with the size of that city.'[3] Others developed the notion that, instead of the crude polarization of urban and rural, there was a rural-urban continuum, only to be obliged to conclude with R.E. Pahl that, 'In a sociological context the terms rural and urban are more remarkable for their ability to confuse than for their power to illuminate.'[4]

Long before the immense changes in rural life of the last forty years, a pre-war survey in Scotland compared verbal ability scores in three regions: the four cities, the industrial belt and rural areas. The mean scores, urban and rural, had little statistically significant difference. Early post-war studies, like that of 11-plus candidates in Cambridgeshire in 1955 and a 'follow-up' survey of Scottish children in the previous year, showed, however, that a majority of high scorers were from urban areas and a majority of low scorers in rural areas, in verbal (IQ) scores. The researchers tried to tease out the conclusions they ought to derive from their findings. For example:

> There is a popular belief that small classes are better than larger ones because they allow the teacher to give more individual attention to each child. Despite this, many parents of rural professional groups prefer to send their children to town schools often at considerable expense. The Cambridgeshire Survey studied this paradox by constructing a table comparing the number of grammar school places obtained by rural pupils according to the size of school which they attended. The results suggest that the smaller schools, mainly rural, obtained fewer places than might have been expected, while the larger schools, which were situated mainly in the towns, obtained more places.[5]

The most extensive of post-war surveys of this kind, based on an urban-rural division of children, was a by-product of the Population Investigation Committee's study of the development of children born in one week of March 1946 throughout Great Britain. The educational progress of the people involved in this long-term survey was studied by the National Foundation for Educational Research. Their findings underline Professor Pahl's scepticism about the sociological usefulness of the terms urban and rural:

> When the results are analysed, rural children are found to be lower scorers than the town children if the groups are separated according to where they lived. When, however, the analysis is carried further and pupils are grouped according to the occupational status of their family, the crude rural-urban differences tend to disappear. A comparison of the urban and rural professional groups reveals that the difference between their mean scores is negligible; a similar comparison of rural and urban manual groups likewise shows little significant difference. However, when the mean score of the combined urban and rural professional groups, is compared with that of all those employed in manual occupations there appears a

significant difference with the former achieving the higher mean scores.[6]

In 1975 the education department in the county of Kent tested all its second-year junior pupils with the appropriate NFER reading test and analysed the results according to its definition of urban and rural locations and according to the size of the school. Small schools were those with up to 120 children; medium, those with 120 to 300, and large schools with more than 300. 'Neither girls nor boys did their best in the small schools. Girls did their best in medium schools. Boys did their best in large schools. As far as the location of the schools was concerned, it was found that boys functioned better in urban rather than rural schools, whereas girls functioned better in the rural rather than the urban situation.'[7]

The Kent findings (derived from over 22,000 pupils) promote interesting speculations but are hardly a guide to educational policy. However, a new level of sophistication was brought to the study of the country child by Derek Twine of the University College of North Wales. He was conscious of all those factors in child development that are not measured by tests of scholastic attainment, and he was aware of the crudity of urban-rural dichotomies. He also realized that rural life was not static and that its 'changelessness' was an attribute of our pervasive romantic nostalgia rather than a characteristic of the real world. He selected part of North Wales which extended from 'urbanised coastal areas with an economy based on industry and commerce, to scattered sheep farms in remote valleys', and divided the catchment area of twenty-nine junior schools into four stages in the process of change, which were 'traditional rural', 'transitional rural', 'emergent urban' and 'wholly urbanised'. Using standard tests and providing Welsh translations, he found that,

The most favourable attitudes held towards school, towards

other people and towards themselves were those of children in 'traditional rural' areas, from communities unaffected by the spread of urbanism. A consistent pattern of attitude levels follows as the community progresses through the phases of the continuum. During the early stages of increasing urbanism (the 'transitional rural' period), there is a marked decline in the nature of these attitudes. Levels build up again to a new 'peak' during the 'emergent urban' phase, although the level attained does not regain that of the original situation. In the final stage of becoming 'wholly urbanised' levels again tend to fall.[8]

Conscious of the importance of personal relationships, particularly with the peer group, in influencing attitudes, Twine circulated parents with a questionnaire to determine the families' progress towards urbanism as a way of life, and applied the 'sociogram' method to the children themselves with the question. 'Think of all the children in this room at the moment. Out of all these people, which *two* would you most like to sit next to, work with and play with?' The plotting of the results of such a question identifies *star* pupils, who are most chosen by their peers and '… therefore embody characteristics which the peers feel to be desirable', and of course it also identifies 'neglectees' (as does any form of social or educational measurement): the people nobody wants to know, or in this case 'those children not chosen even once by their peers'. We learn, with a certain relief, that in terms of individual background factors, 'No consistent pattern emerged; that is, social class, length of residence, distance commuted, etc. were not individually related to pupil-pupil relationships' but that, when these factors were amalgamated into an overall urbanization index, 'In the schools from the "traditional rural" and "emergent urban" areas, there was clear evidence of friendship choices being related to the urbanization index. Also in these phases, in spite of definite friendship groups there appeared overall to be a more compact pattern, with many reciprocated choices and connecting links. At schools in the "transitional rural" and "wholly urbanised" stages, a lack of identifiable friendship groups suggests a total lack of cohesion.'

This lack of cohesion sounds like an implied criticism for the children's failure to make friendships that coincide with patterns set out by sociologists, and Derek Twine concludes that, 'During the period when the rural community is undergoing the initial and major effects of the urbanisation process, the social relationships within the school exhibit no evidence of stars with definite characteristics and no real evidence of cohesion. This is also the period when attitudes to school and schoolwork are at their lowest and when personality characteristics are at their most negative.'[9]

Readers might conclude that he is talking about that well-known phenomenon of adolescence when children get 'turned off' school – some time in early adolescence, and will need to be reminded that this study was made of boys and girls in the final year (aged ten to eleven) of the primary school. Readers may either regret that a similar series of studies was not made in the same area of pupils in the final year of compulsory secondary education (aged fifteen to sixteen) or feel that this kind of attitude-testing has reached its limits. But there are more shocks ahead, for research sponsored by international agencies has shown that one of the limitations on the motivation for educational success among English children has been the concern of parents for the *happiness and wellbeing* of their offspring. This OECD report is not about Calabria but about rural England:

In the areas under discussion there are indications that parents do not always value education, especially beyond the primary stage, as a means of self-improvement or of escape to another sphere. Both they and their children have comparatively modest expectations and there is not that pressure on the children to do well at school which is often noticeable in other, often less agreeable areas. The child's happiness and wellbeing is highly regarded by the parents, and schools are sometimes asked not to push children too hard. This contentment with one's present way of life also makes difficult the persuasion of some children to take up further education courses, especially if it means leaving the area, and schools, quite deliberately, have to give the children a taste of the outside world to spark off ambition in them.[10]

In the actual context of life in contemporary Britain, there are whole layers of unintended paradox about this educational utterance, not the least of which is that similar comments are made about the low-achieving child, whether in small towns where once healthy local sources of employment have vanished totally or in great metropolitan cities themselves. Although we have the stereotype of the free-ranging urban child, we have ample evidence of 'experiential starvation'[11] as a characteristic of inner-city childhood. Trying to come to terms with the rural variety, another OECD report[12] listed the characteristics of rural isolation as:

1.   Initial difficulty in adjusting to the larger social unit which school presents.

2.   Deficiency in the basic skills regarded as normal in a child entering school.

3.   Impoverished language development.

4.   Restricted horizons and lack of experience of the wider society which poses problems of school relevance – a kind of cultural parochialism.

Roy Whittaker and Alan Sigsworth noted that, 'When one studies such a list of the effects which are ascribed to isolation, it bears a striking resemblance to the consequences of growing up in the overcrowded conditions of the inner city and has led one cynic to observe that the social density norm, for adequate upbringing, is presumably that of the suburbs.'[13] Their cynical observer could be right. The suburb is pre-eminently the child-rearing sector of town, and most children, both in Britain and in the United States, are reared in suburbs. So are most teachers. Could it be that in the two extremes – the inner city child and the child who lives deep in the country – teachers do not get the children worthy of them?

Whittaker and Sigsworth sought to examine the perceptions which student teachers held of the rural school and the rural child. Their Pupil-Problem Instrument consisted of a case study of a child causing moderate concern to the teacher. One version read: 'John was fair-haired, blue-eyed and of average height for his age. *He lived in a house at the end of a street with his parents. His father worked on a press in a nearby engineering works.* John was a quiet member of the class, slow in speech and deliberate in his movements. Like several other pupils he seemed to take an unconscionable time to complete the shortest piece of work, kept out of the limelight in Drama and, without any sign of hostility, avoided his teacher's attempts to draw him into conversation by returning monosyllabic answers.'

A second version substituted for the sentences italicized above (but not in the original) the words: 'He lived in a house at the end of a lane with his parents. His father worked as a tractor driver on the nearby farm.' Two further versions substituted the name Susan for John.

The four versions were distributed at random to second-year, fourth-year and graduate student teachers, who were not aware that different versions existed. They were asked to set out in rank order three factors they thought important for the teacher considering this child. The investigators found a much greater readiness to invoke environmental explanations in relation to rural than to urban children, and that their student teachers were 'responding simply to a firmly held stereotype of rural isolation'. If this is the case, they argue, 'It follows that students will enter teaching with an incredibly simplified conception of rural life.'[14]

Children everywhere, we are told, respond to teachers' expectations of them, and I have frequently met the same stereotypes in addressing students on our expectations of the rural child. As a corrective, not to our predictions of educational performance but to those of life performance, I always like to tell them the tale of little Isaac and little Bohuslav, archetypes of the streetwise urban child and of the child who suffers from rural isolation.

Little Isaac, a tax-collector's son, gave his first piano recital at the age of four in Barcelona. 'At seven he was taken to Paris, where he sailed through the entry examinations for the Conservatoire, tossed a ball through one of its hallowed windows and was refused admission, officially on account of his extreme youth. Nothing daunted he became a vagabond, running away from home and from the Madrid Conservatory a year later, and supported himself by his piano playing – chiefly in a vaudeville stunt with his back to the keyboard using the backs of his fingers, palms upwards.'[15] Wandering through Spain as a travelling entertainer, at thirteen he stowed away on a ship bound for South America and worked his way through the towns and cities from Buenos Aires to Havana. Then, on his own, he toured the United States, from New York to San Francisco, wherever there was a piano to play, returning home, still in his mid-teens, giving concerts on the way in Liverpool, London and Leipzig.

Little Bohuslav was the son of the cobbler and keeper of the church tower in the village of Policka on the borders of Bohemia and Moravia. Born in the family's one-room apartment at the top of the tower, he lived there until he was eleven, and spent hours looking out over the endless rural landscape, 'boundless space where the sky kept changing as regularly as nature did below', he wrote years later, evoking the way that '... expanses of winter snow

changed into russet fields, green patches and blue forests
... so firmly planted in the memory that I know them all to
the last detail'. His biographer explains that, 'Bohuslav was
a frail child. He was always ailing and had to be carried
everywhere. Consequently he rarely left the tower and was
brought up in a prison-like atmosphere, isolated and
ignorant of Policka and the human world below ....
Bohuslav found it hard to believe that other people existed
apart from his parents. But his energetic father was far too
busy to play with him and from his domineering mother he
gained little love or warmth.'[16]

His first contact with the outside world was when, 'From
the age of seven he climbed the 193 steps down to street
level to attend school and to take violin lessons with the
local tailor.' Thinking that he had the makings of a virtuoso
fiddler, the citizens clubbed together to send him to the
Prague Conservatory from the age of sixteen. There, alas,
he distinguished himself by his 'incorrigible negligence'.
He '... clashed with academics, both at the Conservatory
and at the Organ School, where he enrolled after being
expelled from the former institution'. Then he 'lived a
bohemian life in Prague, composing prolifically ...'.[17]

If either of these composers had happened to be a child
in Britain today, he would certainly qualify for the attention
of the local authority. Little Isaac would obviously be seen
as one of those hyper-active city kids taken into the care of
the local authority since they are beyond parental control.
(In fact, his father did manage to get him arrested in Cuba,
but he talked his way out of it.) Unquestionably his habit of
escaping would lead to his eventual incarceration in the
Orchard Lodge Secure Unit in South London (euphemis-
tically called a Resource Centre), where points earned in a
Behavioural Modification Programme could earn him
limited access to a musical instrument.

Little Bohuslav, marooned up there in that tower, would
undoubtedly be regarded as a victim of rural isolation of an

extreme kind. His home circumstances were so unsatisfactory that the Director of Social Services would surely seek to find a formula to remove him from so unsatisfactory a childhood environment.

Both these musicians were predictable educational failures. Biographers say that Isaac Albéniz was 'unteachable' and that, 'His handicap was a fundamental lack of self-discipline.' Similarly they explain that Bohuslav Martinů failed in everything. They reproduce the certificate he eventually gained from the Prague Conservatory 'registering his incompetence in every subject – except his ability to teach'. When he later re-entered the school, 'It took him less than a year to discover that he still loathed academic discipline.' The predictions of environmentally conditioned educational under-achievement have been proved to be absolutely right.

It seems almost irrelevant to mention that Isaac and Bohuslav both became world-famous composers, but since they did, wouldn't we predict that Albéniz would produce sophisticated cosmopolitan music in an international style, while Martinů's works would be redolent of his native fields, woods and streams? In fact, the work of Albéniz is manifestly Spanish, '... and the Moorish rhythms, harmonic traits and ornate decoration of Andalusian music was what he most loved to reflect in his own'. And the incorrigibly negligent Martinů left over 400 works. Political circumstances made him a wanderer and led him in his later works to write music that evoked his native land, just because of the series of disasters that befell it, but most of his output was in an eminently cosmopolitan and *avant-garde* idiom like that of *Les Six* in France and Kurt Weill in Germany, as well as 'some of the best spoof-jazz ever written by a serious composer'.[17]

The moral of the story is that there are other dimensions to the child than educational performance, which is a poor predicter of achievements in life.

6 What Teachers Say

They are extremely ill-supplied with subjects to think about.
George Bourne, *Change in the Village*, 1912

My first shock came when one 12-year-old, diagnosed as educationally sub-normal, but struggling one-to-one with me and very keen to write stories, asked me how to spell 'chainsaw'. Such an unlikely word jolted my memory. I asked him what his story was to be about, and withstood a garbled version of *The Great Chainsaw Massacre*, which he had seen on video.
Margaret Underwood, Stoke-by-Nayland Middle School, Suffolk, in
The Times Educational Supplement, 1 August 1986

Most country teachers are well aware that the children in their classes today are not at all like their parents or grandparents who sat in the same schoolrooms forty or sixty years ago. 'I'm actually at a disadvantage,' a Shropshire teacher told me, 'because I didn't see the television programme which they had all analysed to extinction on the school bus before I even met them today.' Another, from Herefordshire, remarked ruefully that, 'They're better informed than I am about the horrors of the contemporary world.'

All the same, when I put to very experienced teachers who had worked in a variety of schools, urban and rural, the question, 'Is there any difference between town and country children?', they all insisted that there was still a recognizably rural child.

Keith, a senior teacher in a secondary school which drew its pupils from sixteen different village primary schools, claimed that 'I know where they come from the moment they open their mouths.'

'How?' I asked.

'By the way they address you, by their general demeanour. I always guess right which village they have come from. Sometimes they lose these tell-tale signs very quickly, but sometimes it stays with them all through their school life here and when you meet them as adults they still display the same characteristics. A lot of country people are very self-contained and wouldn't be changed by an earthquake, let alone the experience of school.'

A teacher in Norfolk who had come there from Birmingham expressed a common feeling when he said,

> Like everyone else, I had developed a certain bright-and-breezy, jokey teaching style that town kids responded to. City children are 'sparky' and quick to respond. When I first came here and taught that way it went down like a lead balloon. No response. Well, of course, it's disconcerting, and it's ever so easy to conclude, as I did, that they were as thick as two planks. I soon lost this urban arrogance because in fact they *were* taking everything in. They just weren't revealing themselves or their opinions. Later still I learned that this is an inborn habit among Norfolk farm families. They have a long history of keeping their opinions to themselves. And of course these children knew a great deal that I didn't know. Not about natural history so much as about the industrial processes of farming, sugar beet and the sugar factory and so on. They know a great deal more than they let on.

Kate, a Suffolk primary teacher with thirty years experience in the same area – so that she really is in the position of having taught the parents of today's children – when asked about the difference between town and country children, instantly replied, 'The urban child is *sharp* but with the country child there's a *steady warmth*. The urban child is "very well stimulated", but with the country child there's a "hug and cuff" culture which is important because Suffolk people do involve their children in their family life in ways that town families don't, even though the father will spend much of his time outside the home in the farm.'

A retired Lincolnshire teacher stressed the same thing: 'In the good old days, farm workers hardly saw their children during the week. The worker got up when they were still asleep and came home after they'd gone to bed. Nowadays he spends most of his time in the cab of a lorry or a tractor, especially as more people earn their livings driving in trades dependent on agriculture rather than in farming as such. All through the school holidays you'll see one of the children in the cab with him. "Going out with me Dad" and "Looking after the van" gives children status in a way that doesn't happen with work in towns to nearly the same extent.'

In her Suffolk village, Kate saw positive advantages in the fact that children learned and played together in a wider age-range than would happen in town. 'It's like measles, they all go through a series of crazes and enthusiasms together. We see them all: rounders, Monopoly, church-bell ringing and discussion groups. Most kids go through a religious phase too ....' Take, for example, the culture of the pub: 'Country children are weaned on home-made wine and home-brewed beer, and as soon as they are able they move on to the pub. The kids are there as locals, everyone knows them. They are among friends. It's a good way of learning. If you want to know about drink it is just as well to do so in a sheltered situation. It's very different from the anonymity of city life.' But even today, she felt, country children are more naïve: 'They wear the same make-up but it is less assuredly worn.'

Another teacher from the same district made the same point: 'We actually have our punks. They're a bit pathetic and a bit behind the times, and everyone says "I don't know what the world is coming to", but there's a kind of desperation about their protest against the timelessness of everything, the way nothing changes very much. No-one will give them a lift, so they have to get the bus to Ipswich or Colchester just to sit around in the Cornmarket or Trinity Square, just to be amongst others with the same symbolic rejection. The majority try hard to chase after other, more acceptable, styles in fashion and the urban youth culture.'

George, the retired Lincolnshire teacher, remembers the implementation in the 1940s of the 1944 Education Act which ended the all-age village school and promised Secondary Education for All:

> People round here were worried because they felt sure that their children would 'grow away' from them at 11 instead of at 14 or 15. They were right and it was a very good thing too. It's a paradox that when farming was in decline it found ways of employing people, while once it entered the post-war prosperity, it has got rid of jobs continually, year after year. Nobody brought other industries to the village and the journey to secondary schools in the town was often the first introduction to a world which in those days held the promise of jobs in which school leavers could instantly earn more in a week than their middle-aged fathers. It was an absolute liberation.

John, after a lifetime of teaching in Norfolk, Suffolk and Essex, revealed a bit of the folklore of teachers which revealed their working hypothesis on the facts of rural deprivation: 'If they're on the bus route, they're more intelligent.' For even in the days when country bus services went everywhere, and before the school bus emerged as what one teacher called 'the lifeline held out to the country child', there were places where the buses did not go, where the rural child was not a village child but lived up the lane off the road that led to the crossroads that the bus passed by.

John's wife Jean, with a similarly impressive record of teaching in every kind of school, commented that, 'If you look at it from the standpoint of the girl or boy, you can see that there are three great dramas in their relationships with the outside world: leaving Mum and going to school in the first place; the immense trauma of leaving the "small" school and going to the "big" school and then finally leaving school itself.

Just because of changed expectations and the changing character of the rural population, these dramas are thought to be harder to cope with today than in the past. Thus Christopher Saville of Suffolk Education Department told an international conference that,

> Infant teachers generally are currently voicing the opinion that children are coming into school less able to cope with the accepted early skills. Concurrently the teacher is having to deal, maybe for the first time, with the son or daughter of the professional newcomer, who has read every article on education that has ever appeared in the Sunday Colour Supplements. If the latter has aspirations for his child in terms of what the education system should provide for him then at the same time the school has got to cope with what one could only call the low expectancy of some parents. It is often a matter of ribald humour when one refers to the 'turnip syndrome' of East Anglia. There is ample evidence to show that the number of pupils, even with the influx of professional and semi-professional people, that take up sixth form places and the number of university entrants tends to be below the national average.[1]

Teachers' explanations of this vary according to temperament. Some fall back on the old argument that over the generations families with ambition and with that 'get up and go' spirit have long since got up and gone. Even E.F. Schumacher, famous as the author of *Small is Beautiful*, after working on a farm for eighteen months during the war, confided to a friend that, 'For generations there has been going on a process of "negative selection". The best have left the land and the dullest stayed behind. The rural population of today strikes me as less enterprising, less adaptable, less efficient, less methodical than the town population.'[2]

As with all such mythologies, people who believe in this generalization have their favourite anecdotes to prove it. Others have learned exactly the opposite, admiring the resourcefulness and the practical and, above all, communal, skills that the education system fails to measure: 'After a life engaged in farm and outdoor work, C, a heavy, gentle man of few words, moved quietly and deliberately about his countless chores. He had the habit of coming by when he saw you alone and in need of company. He'd stand right up there next to you in silence but close enough to make you feel good. Eventually he'd murmur a few inaudible words and beat his retreat home.'

This is one of a series of pen-portraits of his neighbours by Denis Pym, which he uses as exemplars of those characteristics he sees as really useful in a post-industrial world. 'It is in the competent performance of their tasks in relation to other people that their example provides a model for others.'[3] Here is another:

'If there's one person in the village who'll vouch for S's helpfulness and quiet optimism there'll be a hundred. If you're in a fix with ploughing, cutting, unsticking a tractor or in need of a whole range of farm produce, he's your man. S is a solid blustering character and he's also a bit of a lad, which makes him popular with all kinds of people. He's everywhere and in everything – ploughing the field next door, delivering spuds to some old lady in Pound Lane, charging off to Norwich in his white van, the centre of the village hop on a Saturday, or buying drinks at The Parrot. He's the focal person of a large, close-knit family. You get some impression of the extent and meaning of that family at hay making, potato picking time or in S's poultry shed, thick with feathers, just before Christmas, where he's got up to a dozen relatives of all ages preparing the birds with energy and purpose.

I read Pym's collection of exemplars to a meeting of rural teachers at Bury St Edmunds, and their comments were interesting. Some said that they were all recognizable among the parents they encountered; others said that you could recognize among any generation of boys and girls those who would grow up to be each of these types of people, and that, furthermore, they were not pupils of any academic distinction. They flourished in the primary school with its intensely personal relationship but (I was assured) were lost in the atmosphere of the secondary school. Teachers referred me to a novel by a local primary head which, they thought, reflected the early years of these quietly competent people.[4]

The transition from the primary to the secondary school is, thanks to the centralizing policies of local education authorities, a cultural shock just as dramatic as the original shift from home to school as the focus of a child's life. 'Can you imagine', David, the head of Aylesbeare Primary School in Devon, asked me, 'what it means to go from my school, with thirty-one pupils, to the secondary school, which has 2,750?' Like, I trust, the head of every other 'feeder' school, he arranges a series of visits in the last year of primary education, to acclimatize the children to this great move. They settle in.

But many teachers have told me of the 'turn-off point' where rural secondary pupils reject what the school has to offer because they see their future lying somewhere else. It is a common experience that the child who gained a reputation as one of the fourth- or fifth-year 'thickies' seldom caused any trouble and was never caught glue-sniffing on the hillside but tacitly rejected all efforts to involve him in the school's extra-mural activities and was just patiently waiting for what he saw as 'real life' to begin.

'I'm happy to say,' said a Suffolk head, 'that our least promising leavers from last summer have all landed a job in the packing station or the timber yard, or stacking the shelves in Tesco's. What is the point of deploring that these aren't the kind of jobs the careers teacher had in mind? The ones we actually have to worry about are the middle range who didn't pick up much in the way of GCEs and CSEs, don't know what they really want to do in life, and aren't going to make much of further education.'

Kay is a Northamptonshire teacher who sees a particular kind of child almost unaffected by the experience of school:

> The parents are small-holders, transport contractors or general dealers, often a bit of all three. The children are involved in the family business very early in life, they are never any trouble and they seem to drift out of school rather than to leave with any drama or any discussion of job prospects, picking up a living in the margins of the economy along with other members of the family. It's fine for the boys who pick up driving long before they're old enough to have a licence. But the girls have a very thin time in this rough-and-tumble world. Their aspirations for smartness and glamour, or for a job where you can wear decent clothes and keep your hands clean are ridiculed at home, and even at school are often seen as frivolous.

She has often heard fellow teachers discouraging the ambition to become a hairdresser or a shop assistant in Boot's, when the job itself epitomized an escape from mud and grease, oily rags and improvisation. 'The boys are interested in everything mechanical and are quite often very competent very young. We call them little old men because they stand around arguing about tractors and carburettors. But what girl wants to be known as a little old woman?'

Growing Up
in the Country

7 The Culture of the Bus

'Hurry up. You drive me crazy.
Why do you have to be so late?
I wake you early but you're so lazy.
You know damn well the bus won't wait.
Do take your coat. It won't stay sunny.
Take your comb to do your hair.
Did you pick up your dinner money?
Run. You haven't a second to spare!'

Rush down the lane and up to the corner.
If it's gone what do I do now?
Panic makes me get even forlorner.
I'm going to get in an awful row.
I feel quite sick and my heart is drumming.
I'm crying. Where's my handkerchief?
Then suddenly I hear it coming.
I wipe away tears of relief.

Seven hours later homeward we crawl.
The driver dawdles round every long lane.
I'm so impatient that I could bawl.
Aching to be home again.

Fourteen-year-old, 'The School Bus', 1985

When schooling became compulsory in the late nineteenth century, there was already a network of village schools run by the established Church and its Nonconformist rivals, and by private individuals. Boys and girls walked very long distances to get there and back. Custom decided the leaving age, but slowly this was fixed, and over many years it was raised from twelve or thirteen to fourteen until, after the Second World War, it became first fifteen and then, in the 1970s, sixteen.

Those who were destined for the grammar school in the nearest town benefited from the network of railway branch lines which stayed almost intact until they were decimated after the Beeching Report of 1963. An older generation of rural children remembers not the bus but the train and tells stories of the way that, if the engine-driver missed them on the station platform, he would wait for them at the level-crossing, sounding his piercing whistle. Part of the initial popularity of E. Nesbit's book *The Railway Children* is due to the fact that so many of its early (that is, Edwardian) readers really *were* railway children, familiar with the routines and rituals of branch-line working. Most children envied those who had the daily thrill of a train journey out of the village, but even they were looked down upon by the town or boarding children.

One of Elsie J. Oxenham's popular girls' school stories, published between the wars was about the Hamlet Club formed by scholarship girls from the villages, who were ostracized by the resident 'townies' in the county town.[1] To this day there is a similar distinction between the local pupils of a small town comprehensive school and those who are bussed in from the villages, known as 'oooh-aars'.

Gradually, during the 1920s and thirties, the impact of Government reports on the rural education authorities led to various slowly introduced schemes for post-primary education – senior schools, modern schools and central schools. Writing just before the Second World War, F.G. Thomas commented that,

The local reactions to the new senior schools are interesting to note; usually there is intense opposition at first: the children have 'too far to travel', the children are being 'townified', the local school is 'good enough', 'the rates are going up'. Education officers are now familiar with these and many other criticisms. Patiently they meet the local managers and by persuasion and argument the school goes forward. 'It's twenty years too late' is the frequent comment of the villager after the school has been working a short time. The new school is not only accepted but welcomed. The theory behind this programme is, of course, that in areas of scattered population it is prohibitively expensive to provide teaching facilities in terms of the small units of the village school, and that the existing practice of teaching all children over eleven or twelve years of age in one village class with the head teacher limits the scope of education that can be offered. If, therefore, the senior children (aged eleven years or more) are brought to a centrally situated school they can be grouped into reasonably sized classes, and housed in a school adequately equipped and with a well qualified staff.[2]

Here is the whole argument for school buses, never conceived in those days as appropriate for the primary school child, except for really isolated places. With the war came the Education Act of 1944, promising secondary education for all and requiring local authorities to prepare development plans for building, closing or expanding schools. As a result the county councils, through their education departments, became a crucial deciding factor in the provision of rural transport. As Malcolm Moseley puts it, 'Essentially, the local education authority must ensure the provision of, and pay for, adequate transport for all children living more than three miles from school (two miles in the case of children under 8 years). Discretionary powers allow the local authority to do likewise for shorter trips .... The Act also marked the introduction of a pioneer "standard" into rural transport planning ("all children living over three miles from their school shall have free transport as a right") – perhaps a generously high standard of provision which might sit uncomfortably with standards in other fields of rural transport if ever these are developed.'[3]

Dr Moseley's comment is wise. This statutory requirement could have profoundly influenced transport policy for every adult as well as children, making train or bus services viable because they were inevitable. But, through the accidents of the way in which education is financed, they have usually chosen not to decentralize transport but to centralize education. The point was scarcely noticed in the 1950s, when, as new or adapted secondary schools were opened, the increased movement of older children coincided with the 'golden age' of rural public transport. The branch-line network was still intact and bus services were cheap and plentiful. Then the expansion of private car ownership, from 3 million in 1951 to 12 million in 1971, eroded the viability of public transport. Its decline was far more severe in country than in town. Almost all the railway stations closed by the 'Beeching Axe' in the 1960s were in rural areas. 'The level of car ownership and usage in rural areas reflects both the relatively poor provision of public transport and the need of country people to travel to centralized facilities and services.'[4]

As the proportion of school children that could be transported on scheduled public services declined, education authorities complied with their statutory duty by providing a fleet of exclusively school buses of their own or by contracting the service to an independent operator or by making a similar arrangement with a taxi or car-hire firm. Often the same authority will use a combination of all three, according to the locations of the children to be transported. These arrangements are an expense which provides no income at all, since, although the legislation allows school buses to be used by fare-paying adults,[5] they are almost invariably reserved for children with a pass. (Drivers, acting on instructions, will often exclude schoolchildren who happen to be visiting a pass-carrying friend.) The opportunity to extend the facility to other rural passengers is usually ignored by the very council which may also feel obliged to subsidize ordinary scheduled services. Thus Malcolm Moseley remarked in the 1970s that, 'Schoolbuses are of central importance to the whole rural accessibility question. To begin with, they account for a much greater proportion of county council expenditure than does the subsidy of stage bus services. A typical non-metropolitan county council spends well in excess of one million pounds annually on its school transport service. And, because of its scale and peak-hour nature, the demand for school transport in large part determines the size of the rural bus fleet.'[6]

In the country as a whole most children walk to school, travel by bus at their parents' expense or are driven by parents. 'In towns, few primary and only about 10 per cent of secondary schoolchildren travel free; in the countryside up to 20 per cent of primary and 50 per cent of secondary schoolchildren get free transport.'[7] In 1980 the Government in its Education (No 2) Bill sought to allow councils to charge parents for bussing village children. The clause was heavily defeated in the House of Lords, one of the many arguments against it being the promise of free transport that accompanies every school closure. Some idea of the expense of bussing can be gained by the Government's estimate that the defeated measure would (in 1980) have reduced public expenditure by £20–30 million a year.

Most people accept it as inevitable that children of secondary school age should travel to school. It is the fives to elevens that they worry about, and every school closure adds to their number. The worst of parental anxieties, remembering perhaps their own childhood, is that their fledglings are suddenly exposed, helpless, to the rough-and-tumble ways of the big lads. How will they cope? The second is the sheer time the journey can take, for the bus cannot take a direct route. It meanders around the villages, hamlets and picking-up points, so that the child who is picked up first and dropped last can be in the bus for an hour or more each day. That these fears are not groundless can be seen from the work of Britain's foremost environmental psychologist, Terence Lee. To set up a measure of the effect on the child of bussing is extraordinarily difficult but, 'A major survey carried out by Professor Lee in 1957, covering 57 Devon primary schools, found that children exposed to bus journeys lasting longer than fifteen minutes showed evidence of behavioural problems and poor social and emotional adjustment – particularly in boys.'[8]

Certainly the child whisked away by bus from the age of five, with no possibility of direct contact with home, is in a different situation from the child with older siblings who had often traced on foot every inch of the route to the village school long before making the journey 'officially' as one of the new infant intake. Terence Lee concluded from his several studies of the bussing of rural primary children that,

It is the perceived *accessibility* of the home territory and the mother that is so very different for walking and bus children. In the former case, the child walks of his own volition over what very soon becomes familiar territory. He forms a *schema* of the route which unites the home *schema* with the school *schema* and he knows that, although the walk constitutes a psychological barrier greater as a function of its length, he can cross it at any time during the day. On the other hand, the bus child builds little in the way of a connecting schema. The journey itself is not articulated by action or any form of decision-making on the part of the child nor recorded in his cognitive structure. At best he may register a disconnected set of images but, more important, once the child has been deposited at the gate of the school, the bus disappears for six and a half hours and the main means of home access is removed as surely as the kicking of a gangplank.[9]

He also stresses that the journey is not necessarily a sight-seeing tour of the district: 'Most of the time he is preoccupied with what is happening inside the bus and there is no reason whatever to pay much attention to what occurs outside. The acquisition of knowledge about the passing scene is of no functional relevance to the child.'

Most parents, from their knowledge of their own children, would agree with his findings but would suggest that the experience differs as the child moves up the age range. Clare, a rural primary teacher in Herefordshire, told me that, 'At week-ends the boy or girl goes in the family car or by bus, straight along the main road to town for the week's shopping. But the school bus wandering around the pick-up points makes them more aware of the local topography in a way that wouldn't happen otherwise, now that they aren't expected to walk everywhere.' Another, from East Yorkshire, put it even more positively. Kevin said: 'I often think that the bus is the real educator. There's an endless chatter and babble that drives the driver mad, but it is part of the process of self-education through obligatory conversation with other children. They talk and talk, and pick up an incidental education, just like the rest of us do, through exchanging information with their peers. Even the aristocracy on the back seat, the comprehensive kids, exchanging smokes and homework, prepare the primary kids for the wider world.'

However, many teachers and most parents are unhappy to see that the tone of the twice-daily journey is set by the most disaffected and disruptive of the passengers. A series of incidents on one Suffolk school bus, including the occasion when a child lit a fire on the top deck, led the school transport sub-committee to put an escort on board for one term. Concern rose again when the escort was withdrawn, and one member said, 'I believe parents have offered to supervise the bus, but that has been turned down because they are not employed by the county council. The children on the top deck have been very disruptive and causing some anxiety to the driver. This did not happen when it had a supervisor.'[10]

Even more anxiety is caused to parents who live within the minimum walking distance from school but whose route is along heavily used main roads. Continual appeals are made for education authorities to use their discretionary powers and are continually resisted on grounds of expense. The parents of one five-year-old who was the only child in the immediate locality were told when their appeal was turned down that it would cost some £2,400 a year to transport the one child.[11] Transport costs are subject to escalations, particularly in the price of fuel, but Terence Lee warns that, 'It is as reprehensible to argue now that the cost of school transport is outstripping the cost of refurbishing village schools as it was in the past to argue the reverse.'[12] There are more important educational, social and personal issues. The parents of Easton Royal primary school in Wiltshire sum them up thus:

Dependence on the school bus for transport makes it very difficult for children to participate in extra-curricular activities. One of the main arguments in favour of bigger schools is that they offer a greater variety of such activities, but many children who rely on bussing cannot take advantage of any of them. Contacts between parents and teachers are drastically reduced when the child travels to and from school unaccompanied by mother or father. The school itself receives less parental and community support, both in fund-raising and voluntary assistance, because parents and villagers feel less involved with a school they rarely see and, in any case, often have no means of transport to attend school functions. In bad weather children may be cut off from school for several days at a time. This can be disruptive for parents as well as for children.[13]

But what do children themselves feel about dependence on the school bus? My impression is that, with their usual resilience, they accept it as one of the facts of life.

'I was terrified to start with, and scared of the other kids, but I soon found a "protector" who lives round here.'

'Apart from the nightmare of missing it, my big fear was what to do if I wanted to pee.'

'I was like everyone else. I started up at the front near the driver and edged my way further back every year.' Many mentioned this order of precedence, and the way that having an older schoolfellow from the same village could win an earlier promotion.

'Some people graduate from the front to the back. The quiet ones stay in the middle.'

'It was both boys and girls at the back. You have to remember that some people were on that bus for eleven years, dropping off at the primary school for the first six of them and staying on for the high school for the rest of the time. They knew each other since they were infants.'

'There was less pretence down at the front where you just talked about last night's telly. It was the hard and fashionable community up at the back.'

The driver is important too: 'Some we knew very well. Some did nothing but grumble. Some didn't mind if you smoked. One would just stop the bus until people stopped.'

Seasoned travellers are also connoisseurs of the small fleet of coaches run by the bus operators. Naturally it is the oldest vehicles that are normally used for the school run, but sometimes the contractor has to use his most luxurious coach normally kept for Continental tours: 'When the old Bedford that could hardly manage the hills finally broke down, we had luxury travel for a fortnight.'

'One thing that made us different from the town kids was that teachers couldn't give us detentions as we'd miss the bus home.'

'They could always tell the country kids because of the amount of clobber we had to carry around in case it rained or snowed.'

8   Dens and Dams

'We make little squares with dead grass,' writes a Scots girl in the Border
Country, *'and leave a little doorway in one side. We put dead grass in a circle
against one wall as a fire and put rowans in it for burning coal. We hunt
stones to serve as sideboards and dressers. A piece of heather and brown
bracken is put in a corner as an ornament. We take up our old dolls as babies.
Then we pretend a baker arrives in a van. We go out and buy a cake, bread,
and biscuits. Sometimes we go and visit one of our neighbours, make up a
row, and not speak for a few days.'*
Iona and Peter Opie, *Children's Games in Street and Playground*, 1969

Playing house is the most universal of all children's
pretending games. They do it everywhere, in town and
country alike and throughout the world. The author of the
Turkish epic *Memed, My Hawk* from the remote Taurus
highlands of Anatolia, explains how Memed and his
childhood sweetheart Hatché would go off by themselves
and invent new games: 'Among the boys Memed built the
best doll's house, and Hatché decorated it the best.'[1]

A private place is one of the most important needs of
childhood, and the Opies were right to comment that, 'In
our continual search for efficient units of educational
administration we have overlooked that the most precious
gift we can give the young is social space; the necessary
space – or privacy – in which to become human beings.'[2]
When I asked Gemma, a sophisticated twenty-year-old,
what it had meant for her to move at the age of five from
country to town, she instantly replied, 'We found to our
horror and amazement that there was nowhere to have a
den.'

The most famous of all evocations of childhood manipulations of space is Richard Jefferies' *Bevis*, though I have never met a child who finished reading it. This Victorian three-decker novel is very long by modern standards, but Henry Williamson thought it one of the finest boys' stories in our language. He urged that, 'This magical book should be given to boys and girls at the age of ten, and they should be advised to persevere through the early chapters, in order to enter a world they will never forget.'[3] The woods around Jefferies' father's failing smallholding outside Swindon, and Coate Reservoir with its brooks and streams (it had been formed to feed the Wiltshire and Berkshire Canal), provided the setting for inexhaustible fantasy and adventure.

Half-way through the book, Bevis and Mark build their hut, and Jefferies gives very precise indications to his readers on how to set about it. A row of holes were to be dug a foot apart to take long poles which were to allow rafters to slope down to a height of six feet above the ground. 'That would give the roof a fall of two feet in case of rain. Two stout posts were to be put up with a long beam across, on which the outer ends of the rafters were to rest. Two lesser posts in the middle were to mark the doorway. The roof was to be covered with brushwood to some thickness, and then thatched over that with sedges and reed-grass. The walls they meant to make of hurdles stood on end, and fastened with tar-cord to upright stakes .... A piece of old carpeting was to close the door as a curtain ....' After days of work, it was finished and they set about furnishing and provisioning the hut. 'It's splendid,' said Mark; 'we could live here for years.'[4]

Siegfried Sassoon echoed Bevis's adventures on Coate Reservoir in the more modest private world of the pond in the woods: 'When I had enough of fishing I would become busy, improving the shores of the pond. At the end where the water trickles away under the hedge, someone had once made a dam with stakes and pieces of plank; enough remained to prevent the water running away too much. I called this the lagoon, and it had a thriving waterside population of water-boatmen and water-beetles. Minnows, alas, were absentees, but frogs were to be found there. The pond also contained rich deposits of white clay with which I made a snug little port, with jetties and roadsteads and the lighthouse and coastguard station a bit farther round the bay ....'5

He writes with the same detailed animation of the den he had helped his older brothers build: 'The fort had two storeys and was nearly fifteen feet high at one end. It had started as a low shanty among some old laurels and the second storey had been interwoven with them and the middle branches of a mountain ash. Poles, planks, sheets of galvanised iron, and a disused cucumber frame had gone to its making. The second storey was a cabin with one small window and the cracks filled in with putty. To get on to the roof one clambered up a ladder fixed to the outside. There was a little windmill which clattered merrily while the whole edifice creaked and swayed with the trees, so that we felt as though we were on a ship.'

After the adventure of building, his brothers lost interest in the fort, but Siegfried found it a refuge to be alone and feel poetical. Finally he reluctantly agreed that the structure should be burned down to celebrate the new century and, '... its brief glory consumed .... But even if I'd stopped to meditate, I don't suppose I could have realized that the sparks were flying upward from those few years of the departing century which I was able to remember.'6

There was the same immediacy and urgency when Camilla Campbell resolved to build a house in the woods in Norfolk in the First World War: 'We fetched the longest of the great flat fan-like fir branches and placed them against the ridge-pole. The fir branches were very long and heavy to pull out and quite hard to drag across the 20 to 30 yards to our ridge-pole: Bobby and Oscar came to help when they saw what we were doing, but at first they thought it was a rotten game.' It was explained that they needed a house because the Germans were coming and they could all live there. 'We'll have a fire and cook things.' The den-building urge then overcame them all:

Now we could not work fast enough, socks tumbled down, hair got in our eyes, but the boys were quite content to collect the branches, and Helen and I began to build. Choosing the longest and flattest branches to lay in key positions against the ridge-pole, we formed the skeleton of the house. We could hardly bear to leave our house when it was time to go home for dinner. We came back to go on with the building every day that week. First we thatched in the main fir branches with smaller ones. We became quite skilled at weaving the shiny fronds in and out of the main branches. Then we collected moss to plug the remaining holes. It was quite difficult to find the moss. We could sometimes find it on the path, among the bracken stems; and also in the dry brambly ditch at the beginning of the wood. It was only the feathery moss, which we could pull off in small sheets, that was any use: the sort that held together and filled up the shape of any of the holes in the branches. Now the house was really dark inside ....[7]

But the most intensely felt recollection of den-building comes from an aristocratic childhood, described by Julian Fane. His fictionalized self, Vere, is younger than our other builders. In the year before the Second World War he is seven, almost eight, soon to endure the British upper-class torture of being sent away to a preparatory school. His first house, long ago in the previous summer, was simply a nest in the long grass, where he could lie unseen, waiting for 'the rare delight' of overheard conversation. Then, 'Crude shelters begin to appear about the place, branches resting against the trunk of a tree or a piece of rusty corrugated iron enclosing the angle of a wall

– shelters constructed in an hour or two and hardly occupied as long. Christmas passes, and the holidays with their interruption of Vere's activities. Alone again he idly thinks of houses, awaiting some sign, some impetus.' It comes when Nanny reads him a book called *Settlers in Canada*, and the boy is thrilled by the way that, 'These people in the story, without professional experience and with only limited and natural resources, are about to build themselves a house, a fastness capable of resisting both the weather and attack, in a strange and trackless countryside from which they will have to wrest their livelihood. The significance of it all, like rain in a dry summer, transforms his landscape. It is this, precisely this, for which he has been waiting.'

He combs the countryside for a site and finally settles on a place in the angle between two garden walls:

So begins for Vere a period of activity the like of which he has never known. His heart pulses with a steady and productive excitement. He is stronger and more resourceful than ever before. He glories in the size of his undertaking and the problems that confront him. His entire energy is concentrated on the project, every spare moment devoted to a form of toil connected with it .... Day by day meanwhile, notwithstanding setbacks, the work advances. The stones on the top of the walls are rearranged, levelled and packed with earth. The planks from the summer-house are laid across to make a triangular shelter. This is so low that he excavates the soil, to the depth of about a foot, beneath it. The planks do not fit, their crumbling edges admit the light, and he begins to throw the excavated soil onto the roof. It falls through the gaps quicker than he can throw it. He fetches newspaper and spreads it over the planks. The soil after that remains pleasingly in position: he throws it up by the trowelful: it becomes a mountain. He would like to climb onto the roof to smooth it, but the planks sag alarmingly and he does not dare. At least no chinks of light remain: and when trees and bushes grow on the mountain, how secret his house will be – a sort of natural cavern.

Once he has built the outside wall and hung a sack for a door, he turns to the damp, pitch-dark interior: 'By the light of a candle which he has borrowed from the cupboard in the pantry, he pats down the earth in the well of the floor and fashions a doorstep. He drives wooden pegs into crevices in the stone walls, for his coat and for tools, and makes an insecure shelf on which to keep stores such as candles and matches and biscuits.'[8]

All our child builders face similar problems. The constructional ones they have to solve by trial and error. Provisioning and furnishing have to be done by stealth. Bevis used the tin mug and plate that survived from his infancy, and a few items of cutlery from the kitchen drawer, but not silver ones as they were counted every night. (He also bought sherry at the ale-house, as the housemaid would be blamed if it was missed from the pantry.) Camilla Campbell was reproved by her mother, 'But you can't leave china, even old china, up in the wood.' And as Vere was dragging away his sheet of rusty corrugated iron, he met his father, who asked, 'What the hell have you got there?' while his mother remonstrated, 'But really, you mustn't just take things.' The problem of secrecy brings other difficulties, for the builders are usually so proud of their creation that they cannot bear to keep it from the adults who, when they see the tumbledown shack, are either contemptuous or have to feign delight. But some, remembering their own childhood thrills, are truly pleased.

Geoffrey Haslam is an architect whose particular niche is in environmental education, exploring the uses children make of their surroundings and persuading the professional shapers of the environment of the need for places that children can make their own. Remembering his own succession of dens, hide-outs and camps, built with whatever materials came to hand, he found that these building activities, which developmental psychologists tell us characterize the ages between seven and fourteen, were important for most children and implanted very strong memories. But, 'Considering that they can achieve so much at such an age with no assistance or guidance it seems odd that so few adults ever set about building even the simplest structure. Some time during their development, they lose ability, confidence and motivation to build.'[9]

Haslam selected a group of people who seemed to him to be outstandingly creative in their adult lives, and interviewed them about their childhood. They responded with vivid recollections which were an echo of the literary examples I have quoted. He found that none of them had been brought up in cities, but either in the country or in suburbs which in early post-war years were new and in the course of construction and in that stage in their development when they were full of patches of land which were in a transition between one land-use and another. These areas of 'un-make' or 'no-man's land', eyesores to the adult or official world, were of course rich in potential for children. But a common factor in the childhood environments of these people in their twenties and thirties in the 1980s is that they '... now seem to have been used up as building land, leaving only intensively farmed land with few hedges or wild areas'.

Resourceful children still build dens and dam streams. But unless they belong to families with large gardens, they are victims of the municipal urge to tidy up everywhere and cut each blade of grass or, in the eastern counties at least, to turn every patch of ground to commercially viable use.

Matthew and Tom Clayton, aged eleven and seven, built a tree house in the old apple tree at the bottom of their garden at Sturton-by-Stow, Lincolnshire. Officers from the district council's planning department came to measure it and found that it was 0.4 metres higher than the 4 metres above ground level, which is the limit to which a garden building can be erected without approval, and must be pulled down unless planning permission was obtained. Their father then prepared drawings and a specification and paid an application fee of £45, and their den was reprieved.[10]

Other changes in rural life are more serious for the child whose access to woods and streams was unchallenged in the past. Marion Shoard's *The Theft of the Countryside* did more than any other book to alert the public to the systematic elimination, with public subsidy, of non-profit-making patches of land. 'Already a quarter of our hedgerows, 24 million hedgerow trees, thousands of acres of down and heathland, a third of our woods and hundred upon hundreds of ponds, streams, marshes and flower rich meadows have disappeared.'[11] Optimists believed that the bad reputation farmers were acquiring, the election of a Government that allegedly did not believe in featherbedding industry, and the prospect that Common Market policy would impose quotas on cereal farming, as it has on dairy farming, would slow down this loss. But seven years later Marion Shoard found that the threat was if anything intensifying, as farmers '... sought to ensure that if quotas came their own output would be frozen at as high a level as possible. The expansion of cereal growing during the six years up to 1984 alone was accompanied by the removal of 17,500 miles of hedgerow throughout Britain and the clearance of ninety-three square miles of deciduous woodland.'[12] This affects a whole lot of interests, not least the enormous and growing number of citizens who cherish the landscape, its flora and fauna and the freedom to wander, let alone the rights of children.

The issue of conservation has an ironic twist in its tail. The county planning departments employ conservation officers, dedicated people whose public ideology is of persuasion rather than confrontation. It has to be, partly because they have few powers and partly because farming

interests are strongly represented on the councils. (In
Suffolk, where farmers are 1.2 per cent of the population,
they are sixteen per cent of the county councillors and up
to thirty-five per cent of district councillors.[13]) So the
conservation officers urge farmers to retain their remaining
woods and copses and to renew the ancient art of
coppicing. Their leaflets explain how to coppice and what
advantages there will be, describe how they can have new
planting without cost with the use of MSC labour, and
urge them to rear pheasants for shooting. This they do
with alacrity, anyway. Shooting pheasants and partridges
for pleasure is part of the new agricultural lifestyle, for
farmers whose grandparents in the long years of
depression shot rabbits and pigeons simply out of
necessity. They are now as anxious as any aristocrat about
their game preserves, with brooder houses, feeders and
poison for predators (which of course kills wandering cats).
This means that woods where anyone could once roam are
as jealously guarded as game reserves and are out of
bounds for children, including the farmer's own. Even they
are no longer part of the wildlife of the woods.

9 A Place to Play?

You can never know, unless you start very early on in life, the joys and thrills of exploring the woods. I began this some time before I could make out difficult words like Trespassers and Prosecuted, and by the time I had come to understand such long words the woods had claimed me as their own. It was a paradise for birds, being an out-o'-way sort of place, and by the time I was ten years old I knew the names and had a collection of over twenty different kinds of birds' eggs …. I even had a pheasant egg, and that was a serious offence …. My love for the woods was a great annoyance to my father – he couldn't understand it. With a great park to play in why should a lad want to mope about in the woods? 'The lad's fair daft,' he said ….

Fred Kitchen, *Brother to the Ox*, 1940

Our conventional wisdom ascribes two great blessings to the country child. The first is access to natural objects and processes. A post-war Government report on education in rural Wales spoke eloquently of the benefits of this contact. 'It can hardly be denied,' it claimed, 'that the men and women who live most closely to the great rhythms of the natural world possess a greater integration within themselves than is common among those who live in cities. They are more serene and inwardly poised, less susceptible to fluctuations of spiritual moods and depression of material resources, because their roots are deeper, their primary necessities are assured and their characters have been steadily formed by the influences of nature and the unhurried circuit of changeful seasonal occupations.'[1]

We can speculate cynically, of course, about the authors of these lines in the Welsh Department of Education in

Cardiff, who had little time for nature but were thankful for the Welsh grammar school system as an escape route from the hard and lonely life of the hill farms, or from that of the pit villages in the valleys.

Our great natural historians with their childhood exploration of the wonders of flora and fauna were regarded by their parents and peers as eccentric, unless of course they belonged to the leisured, sporting classes, and most of them would surely be regarded by today's enthusiasts for the conservation of nature as unscrupulous predators. Just as Fred Kitchen's father saw him as 'fair daft', so Richard Jefferies' father was disgusted by 'our Dick poking about in them hedges'. Snaring or shooting hares and endlessly loafing with a gun, the neighbouring landowner used to say of him, 'That young Jefferies is not the sort of fellow you want hanging around in your covers.'[2]

In the eighteenth century the observation of nature was such an unusual pursuit that Gilbert White, curate at Selborne in Hampshire, complained that, 'It has been my misfortune never to have had any neighbours whose studies have led them towards the pursuit of natural knowledge, so that, for want of a companion to quicken my industry and sharpen my attention, I have made but slender progress in a kind of information to which I have been attached from my childhood.'[3] He enlisted help, unusually, from the village children. 'We abound with poor,' he wrote, 'and the parish swarms with children,' so, seeking every detail of the habits of the nightjar, White offered sixpence to his 'intelligent young neighbours' for every story they could bring him of the bird. Celebrated passages in his book record the 'bold boy' who climbed a tall, slender beech and 'though standing on so steep and dizzy a situation' brought down the only egg of the honey-buzzard (an exploit we would hardly approve today) and the 'bee-boy', a poor idiot child fascinated by bees, which were 'his food, his amusement, his sole object'. The single-minded White regretted the boy's deficiency only because it prevented him from communicating his knowledge of the life of the bee.[4]

In our reaction against the sentimental assumption that the rural child is nature's natural historian, we tend to make the opposite assumption. Thus in the 1950s Kenneth Richmond declared that, 'The notion that country children cannot help being interested in their surroundings, may be thought to be somewhat starry-eyed, seeing how utterly indifferent and oblivious most of them seem to be,'[5] and in the 1980s Fraser Harrison remarks that, 'Country children, even those whose parents are members of the dwindling farming community, are hardly less ignorant about their natural surroundings than town children.'[6] Others, of course, would be quick to point out that today more people, urban and rural, know more about flora and fauna than at any time in our history.

The second great blessing we attribute to country childhood is that of access to space: room, as we say, to grow up. Our mental picture is of games on the village green and of the ability to wander endlessly, to hang around in the farmyard and help at harvest time, but above all of the freedom to manipulate the environment, 'larking about' in the hayfield, digging, building dens, climbing trees, hiding in the bushes and splashing in the water. Space in the country, everyone agrees, provides opportunity for the vital kind of play that is based on familiar fantasies.

'How does man survive when urban artefacts are removed? This is a very basic question about life and its interest to children is witnessed by the many stories and myths about the countryside. Examples are: Robinson Crusoe, with ideas of survival and self-sufficiency; Robin Hood, the rich and the poor; Hansel and Gretel, with problems of being lost.'[7]

In comparing the present with the past in this respect, we have to allow for several differences in the circumstances of yesterday's children and today's. The first is that comparisons are being made between two different kinds of rural environment: that of farming poverty and farming prosperity. For generations, when cereal production was abandoned in favour of stock-grazing in whole counties, the pre-war broken-down picturesque landscape with its ruined barns, blocked ditches and overgrown hedges was an ideal habitat both for wildlife and for children's play. It did not matter what they did so long as the gates were closed. In large families from overcrowded cottages, children were obliged to be outdoor creatures, and there were few alternative attractions within the home.

Today's rural landscape has fewer children and fewer places for them. If you see them swarming in part of Wales, you can guess that they are city children from an Outdoor Pursuits Centre. The farmyard itself is no longer a safe place for children. A report from Humberside on rural children's play experiences and preferences says that, 'Most of the children understand that they are not allowed to play around farm buildings but not all understand why. About half the children talking about the matter, assume that they themselves are considered likely to do damage. In fact, farm machinery and toxic pesticides are considered so dangerous that special regulations are in force to minimise the risk to children. A quarter of fatal accidents in agriculture happen to children under sixteen.'[8]

From the same region a teacher describes his disillusionment with the opportunities for children's play in the South Holderness village where he lived, 'huddled in a tight island of buildings surrounded by a huge hedgeless, treeless plain of fields, many over 50 acres in extent, and different from their fellows by the colour of their crops'. He says:

If we imagine children racing across buttercup-spangled meadows and shinning up forest oaks, let's forget it. There are few villages in Holderness with common land and fewer still with access to pasturelands .... There is a conspiracy of silence about the veritable network of paths which once connected villages and farms. They cannot be extinguished. That would bring out the ravaging hounds of the Ramblers from the suburbs. Instead they are ignored and neglected. The only open land was a disused railway line which provided a haven for wild strawberries and gorse and the only place in the parish where the local children could go exploring. But covetous eyes are already upon it and no doubt one day it will be ploughed up and fenced off. Then the children will only have their gardens to play in.[9]

Other teachers, however, also in eastern England, stressed the ingenuity of children in colonizing odd and temporary spaces for play: how the parking area of the sugarbeet factory, once the year's 'campaign' was over, became a cycle track or roller-skating rink, how straw bales materialized from somewhere for every kind of activity, how ropes and old tyres made swings from overhanging boughs. The Humberside survey of children's preferences supported this. Marion Wilford, Marie Havercroft and Alice Akehurst interviewed 176 ten- and eleven-year-olds from nine village primary schools and asked them four questions:

a) When you play outside with your friends where do you like to play best?

b) I want you to use your imagination. If you could choose anything you liked, what would be a really nice place for children to play?

c) What places would you like to play in but aren't allowed?

d) Do you have a park or playground near you to play in?

They found most children delighted to talk about their play and that, 'Their words came tumbling out in a way that painted a vivid picture of their environment.' They learned that, 'Their preferred play place is very different from the adult-provided places in most villages. The survey found that 71 per cent of the children spent some time in play areas but most seem dissatisfied with them. Children will use an easily accessible play place where they can meet friends even when they find that place dull and unadventurous.' And needless to say, they found that, 'Rural children do not have the freedom of the fields.'

But there were other factors affecting the accessibility of places generally assumed to be available to rural children. One was distance from home, another was that some children are not allowed to cross busy roads or play near them, and some indeed were not allowed to get dirty, climb trees or play out of sight of home. 'Bearing in mind that these children are ten and eleven years old, this seems like over-zealous care.' Other prohibitions were serious hazards and the risk of the children being a nuisance, while fields, paddocks and woods are usually out of bounds, '... although children of the owners and their friends will often be allowed to play in such places'.

The usual differences were found in the preferences of boys and girls. Bicycles, for example, were used very differently. 'The girls say they ride around the block with their friends or on the street near their home or to visit friends or family at the far side of the village. The boys ride bikes to get far afield, they have races, but most important they use them for scrambling. They look for the muddiest, most slippery, bumpy track they can find. Most of the villages in the survey have informal tracks of this nature which were used as informal meeting places by the boys.'

Traditional playground equipment was mentioned as a feature in their ideal play area by twice as many girls as boys, the most popular item being swings. However, the home-made rope swing or tyre swing hanging from a tree was suggested more often than any item of traditional playground equipment. None of the girls but two thirds of the boys would like an 'assault course', either one they could make for themselves or one specially provided, with rope swings, ladders, nets, pulley slides, ropeways, walls and forts.

However, it was possible to identify, both from the present activities of boys and girls and from their concepts of ideal places for play, certain features of the 'natural' landscape. Although no questions were asked about trees, they were mentioned spontaneously by fifty-three per cent of girls and seventy-six per cent of boys. They are the most popular play feature of all. They can be climbed and hidden behind; they can become forts or bases; with their surrounding vegetation and roots, they become dens and little houses; they provide shelter, landmarks and privacy; fallen, they become part of an obstacle course or material for den-building; near them you find birds, little animals, conkers, fallen leaves, mud, fir cones and winged seeds; they provide a suitable backdrop for every conceivable game of the imagination. Bushes and undergrowth have many of the same features, valuable for dens, hiding games, cover for war games and a great place for creating tunnels and paths.

Of long grass, corn and bales, the researchers comment that, 'Areas of long grass or, better still, corn and barley can be crawled through on a child's tummy; children see insects and wild flowers as though they are peering through a jungle; they can be hidden in as part of a game or used to hollow out a little place for secrets; mown grass and straw are popular for straw fights; bales are good for dens and jumping and hiding. So popular are corn, long grass and bales, that law-abiding, compliant girls will break the rules to play with them.'

Finally there is water, which, in the children's view, added an extra touch of magic to a play area. The researchers observed that, 'Deep water for fishing or swimming may well present too many hazards in an unsupervised play area, but a little stream has great play potential. It can be paddled in; turned into a moat in the imagination; crossed by means of stepping stones or home-made bridges; and of course children can simply sit and watch the water or ride their bikes along the muddy banks.'

All these homely features of the landscape are taken for granted. They demand no heavy investment by local authority departments of recreation and leisure. But the Holderness teacher was right, in his grim picture, to stress the same point as the Humberside investigators emphasize in their cheerful presentation. They noted the importance of what they call wastefields – pieces of land waiting to be built on or sold or too small and awkward for any conventional agricultural use. 'Several children mention pieces of land where they play at present but which are up for sale.' This is why they warn their colleagues in local playing fields associations that, 'Unofficial play places are lost to children every day and it is as important to campaign against this as for the acquisition of play areas.'

Similarly they urge that such groups should work even more vigorously to create an awareness of the importance of play in the minds of the public, that they should persuade those involved in children's play to spend time consulting the children themselves, and that they should inform parents. For, 'There are so many new dangers in rural areas that many parents simply restrict their children's play opportunities rather than teach them to become self-reliant in their environment.'[10]

Schools Under
Threat

10   Key Villages and Others

Two villages nearby have been swamped by large estates that have completely overrun and obscured the original settlements, and village life as it was known has been lost for ever. Others have experienced the exact reverse, with no development being allowed, meaning that the villages have almost completely run down; at one no new houses have been built for young couples, the population has become aged, the village school has been closed, the shop and pub see little custom, and there is a strange feeling of decay in the air.
Robin Page, *The Decline of an English Village*, 1974

Robin Page's complaint from south-west Cambridgeshire is an illustration of the well-known fact that whatever planners do is wrong, for he is referring to the 'key settlement' policy that has dominated rural planning since the Second World War.

That war, as we have seen, brought a national mood, created in part by the experience of evacuation, that things were going to be different in future, that there was a universal right to certain basic services and that people were not to be penalized for being poor or for living in remote places. One of the means of achieving this aim was to be the post-war comprehensive planning legislation which gave local authorities a theoretically absolute control over new development in town and country alike (with certain exceptions, such as farmers, royalty, Government itself and 'statutory undertakers' of service provision). Professional planners, obliged to prepare originally 'development plans' and latterly 'structure plans', based their approach on the geographical concept known as 'central place theory' which identified a hierarchy of human settlements with a series of threshold populations which determined the catchment area of, say, a post office or a primary school, rising to that of a regional hospital, a university or an opera house.

Central place theory, in the form of the designation of key settlements or key villages, dominated planning policy in the countryside for many years. The National Council of Voluntary Organizations examined twenty-one county structure plans and found that eighteen of them relied on a key settlement policy of concentrating private development and public investment in chosen villages and consequently denying them to others.[1] Slowly a body of opinion grew up, not least among the professional planners themselves, that rejected this universal policy, on philosophical, practical and humanitarian grounds. Philosophically many people cannot accept the idea that local authority officers far away in county hall should have powers over the life or death of places. Thus the American writer Richard Sennett complained that the planners have wanted to take the plan, 'the projection in advance, as more "true" than the historical turns, the unforeseen movements in the real time of human beings.'[2]

The most notorious example of this in British rural history was the saga of the colliery villages of County Durham. Faced with the decline of the coal industry and the continual closure of pits, the county council soon after the war graded the villages from A to D according to predictions or projections made then about their future economic viability. The policy was bitterly opposed by the inhabitants of those villages that in their view had been 'left to die', and there were innumerable public enquiries, demonstrations and reproaches.

In 1972 I visited a primary school due for closure in one of the category D villages, having been asked to comment on the entries for a competition organized by one of the oil companies on how children could play their part in re-shaping their environment. There was an irony in the situation that was not lost on their teacher. She said, 'They're talented, they're bursting with ideas, and they have a loyalty to the place. It isn't even tumbling down. These houses would last forever, but their parents aren't allowed to improve them with or without a council grant. How would you feel?' I remarked that year at a meeting in Newcastle that,

> A village in Category A, like Escomb, has been rehabilitated sensitively and intelligently, without avoidable dislocation in the lives of its people, but Category D villages like Witton Park, with an absolute ban on new buildings and on improvement grants, have been left to die without regard to the wishes of the inhabitants or to changing prospects of local employment. Officially dead, but unwilling to die, the Category D villages have fought for survival. A few have been upgraded, but most have been kept in the condemned cell, even though, as at High Spen, new industry has provided more jobs than the closed colliery. The officials who assumed the role of God in dividing the sheep from the goats have themselves long since moved to greener pastures, but their decisions of twenty years ago remain more 'true' to Durham County Council than the subsequent activities and aspirations of the people who live in the villages sentenced to death.[3]

I was, of course, criticized by the planners but, returning twelve years later, when County Durham's economic situation was much worse, I was told that the first new houses of a lifetime had just been built at Witton Park. Durham was an extreme case, and the late John Barr in his sensitive account of the issues involved concluded that, 'A way of life *is* being destroyed. But for all its virtues, it is not a way of life that can survive. On balance the planners are right.'[4] But policies that could not work there could not work anywhere.

Nor do they. Key settlement policies arouse an enormous local opposition for two opposite reasons. On the one side are the residents of places chosen for expansion. For the operation of key settlement policies *does* work in the sense in which Jon Gower Davies claimed, in that the impact of planning '… is least onerous and most advantageous to those who are already well off or powerful, and it is most onerous and least advantageous to those who are relatively powerless or relatively poor. Planning is, in its effect on the socio-economic structure, a highly regressive form of indirect taxation.'[5] Among relatively poor people who are particularly dependent on the public provision of services there actually has been, as a country clergyman notes, a tendency to …

> move out of the smaller settlements into the key villages. Parents, particularly those without private transport, whose children are at secondary school, are likely to find living in a remote hamlet with almost no public transport links, very difficult, and a significant number have moved to the larger settlements. At the same time, the smaller settlements are a particular popular choice for the retired and second home owners. Thus in certain areas, a pattern of social zoning has emerged in the countryside, whereby the smaller hamlets and villages tend to be populated by the relatively affluent, who are less dependent on the public provision of services and facilities, while the key villages attract those who need ready and frequent access to such services.[6]

This trend does not fit the egalitarian ideology of planning, so it is officially ignored. But it underplays several factors. The first of these is that plenty of people are unable or unwilling to move. Some have that irrational attachment to the place where they live which is considered natural above a certain social level but is sheer pig-headedness if you are poor, as in those Durham villages.

The second is that many of them cannot move anyway, because they are council tenants or rent the house they have occupied for generations or are poor owner-occupiers who could never afford the cost of a house somewhere else.

The third is that among those incomers, apart from those who conform to the stereotype and are determined that the village shall stay exactly as it was when they first happened to see it, are others who, with some knowledge of the way the system works, are willing to use their energy to maintain the village's right to its share of the services taken for granted elsewhere.

The fourth is that every village has children to whom key settlement policies are a hidden threat since they have, surely, a right not to grow up in a museum. In my nearest village, the youth club was wound up in 1980 and the organizer ruefully remarked that, 'If you can buy a house there it is prestigious. It really is a dying village.'[7] Her view was reinforced by that of the county education officer (who, like the Durham planners, has since moved up the hierarchy to become chief executive of another county) as 'a rather dingy room with clapped-out furniture, an old stove spreading its feeble heat through its wrought iron protective barrier, enlivened visually only by the exquisite art work of the youngsters'.[8] Such poetic prose, I thought, indicates a clear intention to close it, with its under thirty pupils and 2½ teachers, the moment the head retires. Planning policy is thus both cause and effect. The 'unspoilt' village with three restaurants but no café has coachloads of appreciative visitors every summer.

Within the planning world there have been years of increasing misgivings about the effect of key village policies which '... were (and still are) seen by most planners as a kind of universal elixir for the multiple ailments of rural Britain'.[9] One consistent opponent, Ian Gilder, stresses that beyond the theoretical arguments the fundamental practical one dominating policy is that there are economies of scale in the provision of public services. He argues that these economies apply to only a few such services[10] and that,

> When the cost curves for all rural services are amalgamated no clearcut relationship between the costs of services and size of village exists. The conventional view that there are distinct population thresholds for particular services is a gross simplification. Over time the cost curves for particular services have changed radically in shape as the relative costs of labour, energy and other factors have altered. In the case of certain rural services, such as sewage disposal, substantial technological changes which have resulted in the introduction of small package plants have upset our ideas as to the most efficient unit size for that service. Many schools, for example, are only operated in a particular way for administrative or political reasons. The change to comprehensive education completely altered the economics of rural services. Similar changes will no doubt happen again.[11]

He maintains that, 'All the economic arguments seem to favour the maintenance and development of the present pattern of dispersed settlements. The lower the rate of growth the stronger become these arguments. No useful savings can be made by concentrating development in a few large villages …. The economic basis of key village policies no longer exists.'

But there is a time-lag between research findings and policy change. Some planning authorities have quietly relaxed the rigidities of key village policy; others have embraced the concept of 'dispersed development' on the principle that the planning unit '… would not be an individual village but a system of perhaps five or six villages over which public services, residential development, educational and employment opportunities would be spread'.[12] Such a policy would at least avoid the crudity of development or stagnation of which Robin Page complains. It might mitigate too the widespread view among village-dwellers that, if the authorities had their way, nothing at all would happen except in towns. In the health service this view is underwritten by the fact that, even if a general practitioner wanted to open a new part-time surgery in the country, he would find that the village was 'restricted' by the DHSS, and in education by the situation such as that in West Dorset, where nearly half the population lives in villages of fewer than 500 people but where seventy-five per cent of these villages have no school.[13]

Yet the moment we abandon the key settlement ideology, we can see that there are dozens of alternative approaches to both public and commercial services.[14] The NCVO's advice is to follow six steps: 'If you have a local service, use it; find out whether local services are under threat; establish partnerships between the community and local authorities; look for combinations of services for mutual support; get the parish council to support voluntary initiatives; and if all else fails, provide the service on a co-operative basis. There are pubs, doctors' surgeries and an isolated shop/garage and post office all owned by parish councils.

In my neighbouring village of Polstead there had not been a shop for ten years until one was opened by a group of local volunteers with small loans from the district and parish councils. Its chairwoman explained to me that they were simply following initiatives in Oxfordshire, Norfolk and Devon, which have been followed by the Gwynfi Co-op in South Wales. She pointed out that, even with the minimal overheads they had achieved, the shop, if run for profit, would bring in only about £50 a week and could thus never provide an income for a trading family. They would have to do it themselves or go without. And she rejoiced that, 'It has indeed become a social centre in just the way we hoped it would, and not only for old people. It's a local focus and it provides our small children with that vital experience of going shopping on their own, handling cash by themselves, and all those other childhood experiences we all used to take for granted.'

Every kind of local service has the same incidental importance in the lives of children, unless we take it for granted that the future function of the village is to be simply that of a retirement colony or dormitory.

11   Should We Save Our School?

For some time after the last war these schools lacked any kind of charm and were even found hateful, as being remnants of an all too easily remembered poverty, both physical and intellectual, and sometimes of brutality. Those who attended them breathed a sigh of relief when they were closed down and their own children bussed to new sunny Primaries miles away. However, as with all things, the day of re-evaluation has dawned ...
Ronald Blythe, Introduction to Jon Wyand's photographs *Village Schools*, 1980

When Ronald Blythe's *Akenfield* was filmed in the late 1970s, the children and their teacher in the village of Charsfield in Suffolk dressed up in the clothes of late Victorian times and acted out their roles of a hundred years earlier. It has been done many times since in celebration of the centenary of the schools built by the School Boards after the 1870 Education Act.

On that occasion one of those photogenic accidents occurred. Teacher, playing her part realistically, admonished one child sternly, and he, never having been addressed like this in his life, burst into uncontrollable sobbing. When the scene was shot, everyone rushed forward to console him and to stress that it was only a game.

It was a reminder that the village school was once a hard and tough environment. Janet Hickman recalled not Victorian times but the inter-war years when she was a sickly orphan shunted between urban and rural foster homes:

Because of my backwardness I was put in the infants' room with Miss King. The other children looked upon this as a disgrace and shouted 'dunce, dunce, double dunce' after me. I had grown very tall for my age and looked older than I was, which did not help my troubles; I dreaded going into the 'big room', where the bigger boys, great farm lads of thirteen and fourteen, used to jeer at me and terrify me. Or so it seemed. It is quite possible they didn't give me a single thought – but they seemed so large, and their voices so loud it was a daily wonder to me when I arrived home in one piece. Life has been made much easier, both for teachers and younger children, since the system of dividing schools into primary and senior became generally accepted. Compulsory education came hard to Norfolk, and these boys and girls too had inherited from their parents, who were allowed to go to work as soon as they had satisfied the authorities they could read and write, a rebellion against sitting in school, being taught a 'lot o' old squit', when they could be earning money.[1]

In the immediate post-war years country parents welcomed the sometimes very belated implementation of the Hadow Report of 1926 which recommended separate schools for seniors, and the slogan of secondary education for all, which, following the Act of 1944, renamed all those senior departments as secondary modern schools. Much later they may have welcomed, if they could understand them, the plans of education authorities to redesignate village schools as 'first schools' or 'middle schools' as a preliminary to even larger and more centralized upper or high schools. The problem was that all these decisions, made far away in County Hall, made the little local school less and less viable. The Plowden Report of 1967 (*Children and Their Primary Schools*), which urged that schools with a five-to-eleven age range should have at least three classes, each covering two age groups, was used as a justification for closing schools which were administratively inconvenient. Eleven years later Lady Plowden herself had second thoughts, admitting that, 'With all that we know today, the policy about village schools needs rethinking.'[2] Her change of perception was ignored, and the opinions of parents, who had assumed for years that the Director of Education must be right, were ignored too, as pressure grew for the closure of small rural primary schools.

Until 1978 it was nobody's business to monitor closures, but research from Aston University suggests that about a thousand rural schools were closed between 1955 and 1967. After the appearance of the Plowden Report, another 660 closed between 1967 and 1974, with about 275 from 1974 to 1980.[3] In 1978 the Department of Education and Science began to compile data, and it finds that between then and 1984 there were 508 closures. This mounting toll was not necessarily a massacre of the innocents. In their superlatively balanced study of *The Small Rural Primary School*, Adrian Bell and Alan Sigsworth note that, 'We were told by one LEA adviser of a headteacher who, when the numbers in his school had fallen to a mere five pupils, had recommended to their parents that the children be transferred to another school. On the opening day of the following term, he arrived to find himself the only person in the building. If you are a rural school, you cannot die more alone than that.'[4]

I was once given a bed for the night in a Welsh household where the windows were full of 'Save Our School' posters in two languages. When I woke in the morning, a minibus called to pick up the children, so I asked my hosts whether they had failed to save the village school. They replied that the teacher was so dreadful that there was no way *their* children would go there. They were bussed down the valley to the school in the next village. I mention this deliberately because education officers in more than one county have used such tales to *prove*, to their own satisfaction, that campaigns against village schools come from sentimental middle-class lobbyists who would not dream of sending their own children there. Research shows that the degree of parental opposition to closure relates closely to local opinion about the head teacher. 'Schools which have lost that parental support, and found their numbers dwindling as a consequence, have, so to speak, died before they have been officially closed.'[5]

When parents carried placards saying, 'Kill our school and you kill our village', the former chief education officer for Suffolk, Duncan Graham, who has since moved on and up in the administrative hierarchy, would claim that this was demonstrably untrue, since villages without a school had gone on growing just as much as those that retained their school. He did not elaborate on the extent to which the incomers were two-car or childless households. The sentiment behind the placards and posters was real enough. Faced by creative accounting that demonstrates that small schools are more expensive per child/year than larger, centralized schools, rural parents often, and naturally, reply, 'But it's all we get.' What they mean by this is precisely what they say: that of all the services provided by the county council's precept on the rates they pay to the district council, or by its grant from central government from the taxes they pay, education is the one service (apart from the tarmac on the roads) that rural residents actually make use of. They argue that those education officers who isolate a cost per child/year to prove that village parents are selfishly demanding more than their fair share of resources, never tell the truth about the village's share of total resources, nor about the cost of bussing, nor about the additional costs of enlargement and additional staffing in those schools selected to receive the children from closed village schools.[6]

Early in this century Edmond Holmes, a famous Chief Inspector for Elementary Education, who had watched an immensity of bad, mechanical teaching for thirty years, wrote a book describing his ideal school. It was a single-teacher, all-age village school (modelled, it is said, on one he had visited at Ringmer in Sussex), with no division of the process of learning into subject areas. The children taught themselves, and each other.[7] Three-quarters of a century later, his lineal descendant in office, Geoffrey Elsmore, Chief Inspector for Primary Education, told teachers that ideally every primary school should have nine teachers for the nine subject areas considered to fit the inspectorate's view of the curriculum.[8] Understandably, ordinary rural parents, knowing their own children, have no such inflated conception of what the primary school should provide. They are humble enough to want their children to be safe, happy, busy, numerate and literate, and they want teachers to be friendly and approachable, not at an annual meeting but in an informal, day-to-day automatic relationship. Assumptions about class and culture made this impossible in the past, when Teacher was regarded with awe or fear. The changed relationship between parent and school is precisely why they are hurt and bewildered at the thought that their hopes for their children cannot be met in their own village.

In August 1986 the Department of Education and Science issued a draft circular to local education authorities that only in exceptional circumstances should primary schools with fewer than sixty pupils or three full-time teachers be retained, because they would lack 'the necessary range and mix of teacher experience and curricular expertise'.[9] That document was widely used by local authorities, just as the Department knew it would be, to justify the proposed closure of this or that school among the 1,500 to 2,000 affected.

On the eve of the General Election of 1987, after the county councils had made their decisions, the Secretary of State withdrew the draft statement, saying that his Department's views were '... not to be interpreted as narrowly prescriptive or as providing a set of benchmarks for the closure of schools'.[10] Having placated the rural vote with his bland statement that, 'I recognize the wide degree of support that many rural schools command within their local communities', the Secretary of State issued a new circular, saying nothing of the kind and urging local education authorities to eliminate spare places since, 'Schools of any size with a substantial proportion of surplus primary places incur disproportionately high unit costs in maintaining under-used capacity.'[11] At one stroke central government was able to apply a financial squeeze onto county councils, feed them with every possible reason for closing village schools and then allow *them* to endure the odium of enforcing unpopular decisions.

In 1986 the defeated supporters of Easton Royal Primary School in Wiltshire produced a devastating pamphlet, *The Conspiracy Against Village Schools*, setting out in detail the misrepresentations and distortions of both educational and financial evidence used to justify school closures.[12] They sent a copy to the Secretary of State, who wrote to say that he was a party to no conspiracy, since it was the local education authorities who closed schools, not him.[13] By the following year he was, like Squealer in *Animal Farm*, taking over the arguments of his opponents, telling the world that, 'Closing a school does not save as much money as you'd think. The local authority has to expand another school or lay on transport.'[14]

Again like Squealer, both the Department and the local administrators change their ground overnight, and the moment local campaigners win one argument, they find new reasons for justifying closure. Teachers are discovered to suffer from 'professional isolation' in the age of instant communications, a disease never diagnosed in rural doctors, solicitors or administrators. Parents are rebuked for their sheer selfishness in denying their offspring the company of a football team's worth of companions of the same age and sex. Subject specialists are discovered to be as necessary in the primary school as in the secondary school. And, as a master-stroke, the Education (School Premises) Regulations of 1981 are evoked to show that the building is not big enough to be viable. Local authorities are selective in using these regulations because of the astronomical cost of adapting all schools to meet them, but, 'Villagers whose school may have held 50 or more children comfortably in recent years, and perhaps up to 100 before the 1944 Education Act transferred the older children to secondary schools, are understandably baffled and angry when told that the building is large enough for only 12 or 13 pupils.'[15]

There is, of course, a hidden agenda in county halls on the strategy of closure. One deciding factor is whether the school's area is represented by a councillor of the party that happens to be in control of the council. Another is how close the head teacher is to retirement or an offer of 'early retirement', and what influential connections he or she might have. Yet another important factor is the extent to which the village has enough parents with the time and sophistication to mount a noisy and visible campaign against closure. Educational arguments are a camouflage for administrative convenience.

But in any case they ignore two vital and obvious things. The first is that it is easier for a teacher to move around between schools than for a busload of unsupervised infants to do so. The peripatetic music teacher is a characteristic of the education system rural and urban, and the Schools Rural Music Association[16] has existed for generations to overcome geographical limitations in that particular (and threatened) aspect of school activity, and exactly the same mobility of specialists can be applied to any other subject area discovered by the inspectorate to be vital.

The second vital thing is the degree of co-operation between village schools. In Dorset, a project called DARSET (Dorchester Area Rural Area Schools

Education Team) links ten first schools in places like Bere Regis, Piddle Valley and Cerne Abbas, to stimulate the work of both teachers and pupils in language learning and creative activities and explorations. 'There were outings to a watercress bed, a bird reserve and a water mill, followed by the chance to choose an activity ranging from baking bread to writing songs.'[17] Another of its initiatives is a play-and-learn bus visiting pre-school children in lonely hamlets and remote farms.

In East Devon three small village schools have all through the 1980s developed their COSS project (Co-operation Between Small Schools), one specializing in environmental studies, another in science and health education, and the third in pottery and craft, with a shared Wednesday afternoon for games. The venture has been carefully monitored and assessed by one of the head teachers involved.[18] In the Eye area of Suffolk, ten small primary schools, all 'feeders' for Hartismere High School, have formalized the informal relationship in sharing resources and staff skills. One primary head, Bob Perrett, stresses that, 'No one tries to dictate what the other schools should do. It is a harmonization for mutual benefit without pressure.'

Adrian Bell and Alan Sigsworth in their study of small schools describe a whole series in north-west Norfolk, Nottinghamshire and Northamptonshire, Cornwall, Powys and Gwent, as well as aspirations for a locally relevant rural curriculum in the Western Isles.[19] But the thrust of their book is not to discuss how much educational experience we should stuff into our under-elevens. Based on hours spent in quiet observation of the classroom scene, it is a gently argued case for seeing the small rural primary school as an educational ideal rather than as an administrative problem. They are concerned with the *quality* of the experience of school, and they demonstrate that the large aspirations for links with the community, for co-operation between age-groups, and for joint activities between schools that fill the rhetoric of educational reports, are actually realized in small rural schools. Accustomed to the rigid age-stratification of large urban schools, we forget how unnatural it is and what advantages there are in an educational community in which '... the junior children do not seem to feel that their status is diminished if they lend support to infant contributions; a joking relationship binds infants, juniors and headteacher together.'[20] Thus, '... both younger and older children benefit from learning side by side. The younger children learn a great deal from watching the older children do things. They try out the ideas for themselves and they also aim higher in their activities .... The older children also benefit in many ways. They watch the younger children reaching stages that they remember going through themselves .... Children love an appreciative audience to listen to stories, admire works of art, watch plays, and enjoy many other activities. The, largely uncritical, younger children help particularly to increase the confidence of the rather shy older children and give them a sense of successful achievement.'[21]

One of the most significant of all pieces of experimental research on the effect of size on school performance was carried out in America and replicated on Prince Edward Island in Canada and on a smaller scale in Cheshire. It found that, 'Students from the large schools *were exposed* to a larger number of school activities and the best of them achieved standards in many activities that were unequalled by students in small schools; on the other hand, students in the small schools *participated* in more activities – academic, inter-school, cultural and extracurricular; their versatility and performance scores were consistently higher, they reported more and "better" satisfactions, and displayed stronger motivation in all areas of school activity.'[22] Since we have all learned by now that motivation is nine-tenths of education, and since the young, urban or rural, live in a culture which, whatever its virtues, is profoundly anti-educational, this finding is one of the most important of all contributions to the endless debate about schooling.

There is yet another factor that explains the passion with which local people defend their threatened school, even insisting, as parents from West Slaithwaite near Huddersfield did in 1987, on taking their case as far as the appeal court, and succeeding on the grounds that inadequate reasons for closure had been given. This is because, however much the idea of the 'village community' is a product of rosy nostalgia, it ensures that the school is seen far more as an asset and responsibility of the local community than many a school elsewhere that is officially described as a 'community school'. People are willing to donate their time or their specialist skills or their money to the school just because it is *their* school. Molly Stiles, national co-ordinator of the NASSS, remarks that, 'It's not just the parents who are contributing in this way. It's somebody's second cousin or the lady who cleans the church who wants to see the village school survive.' And a first-school head from Buckinghamshire surveyed twenty-three village schools with fewer than sixty pupils and found that most had raised funds worth fifty per cent or more of the capitation paid by the county.[23]

In the politics of education, some people object vehemently to this kind of involvement, firstly because it is thought to relieve education authorities of their responsibilities for which the public pays in rates and taxes, secondly because the voluntary work undertaken deprives trade union members of potential jobs, and thirdly because it widens the gap between rich and poor areas.

St Mark's Church of England School at Hadlow Down in East Sussex, with twenty-nine children from twenty families in its roll, gained £2,000 in 1985 alone. When parents at Henley in Suffolk offered to build a new classroom and to meet the greater part of the cost of the materials, the education committee overwhelmingly rejected the proposal after a warning from the chief education officer that 'Other requests from parents associations could follow in the train of this.'[24]

When the spending cuts made by the Callaghan Government caused West Sussex County Council to abandon its proposed two extra classrooms at Angmering, the education committee recommended the acceptance of this 'revolutionary idea'.[25] But when our villages really were poor, there was nothing revolutionary about it. I passed a building in a country town with a stone let in a wall recalling that, 'These two classrooms were built by public subscription on the occasion of the coronation, 1902,' and today illiterate poor parents in the squatter settlements of any Latin American or African city take it for granted that they should build a primary school for their children.

When Buckinghamshire abandoned its school meals service, Rose Cadle, who had been kitchen assistant at Brill Primary School for fourteen years, and Vera Rolfe, who was retiring after thirty years as school cook there, became self-employed and took over the kitchen, selling meals at the same price as before and receiving a subsidy from the authority for those entitled to a free meal. The venture led to a revival of the school garden. 'It was the vicar's idea to grow these vegetables and he got in touch with Johnnie Blaine, who is retired and one of the village's keen gardeners. He is growing the vegetables with the help of the children and, at the same time, teaches them some gardening skills.' After the kitchen has had its share of vegetables, the surplus will be sold to boost funds. Talk of allotments reminded Vera Rolfe that the school had its own allotment in the 1950s and sold potatoes to the county council for the school meals. 'We used to bottle things in those days. The whole school would go out for a nature walk and pick blackberries. People used to bring us apples, gooseberries and rhubarb. We would bottle those as well and, in the winter, put them in pies for the puddings.'[26]

Such stories can be multiplied all over the country. At the Coombe School in Berkshire, everyone participates in the school's garden festival, held at the time when the travelling horse-dealer is around so that he can pass on to the children the secrets of grooming horses. They are a reminder that one of the inestimable advantages of the village school is just that it *is* the village's school.

12   A Rural Curriculum

The teacher (at Kyambe School) is busy explaining something about Rural Science in England. Upon his pointing at a picture on the map, and asking what that particular object is, the whole class roars in chorus – which cacophony our teacher seems to enjoy. Thus we sing that what's denoted is 'Rural sheep', 'Rural Zoo', 'Rural city', 'Rural cows', 'Rural fish', 'Rural sea' .... We all like Rural Science. It sounds very intelligent and it encompasses everything. We wonder why this teacher is not allowed to be our sole instructor for everything. It would be easy and much in tune with our intellectual aspirations. We would have Rural Mathematics, Rural English, Rural Bible Study, Rural Civics, History and Geography. Everything would be simply Rural ....

David Mulwa, *Master and Servant*, 1979

Schooling is an obligatory apprenticeship to life, but to what kind of life? Should the public education system in rural areas prepare children for the careers that were, until well into this century, ordained for most of them: the boys as farm servants for life, the girls as domestic servants until they married and became village wives and mothers, performing miracles of improvisation and economy on pathetically inadequate incomes? Or should it prepare for the great aim of equality of opportunity for all (to become unequal) and ensure that a career is open to the talents of every country child, even though few will succeed?

This dilemma has pursued the whole history of rural education in Britain and has been repeatedly kept alive in all those nations once subjected to colonial rule. It arises because the master-stroke of the education industry has been to ensure that *it* alone provides entry into occupations that are lucrative, devoid of back-breaking physical labour, providing high status and that wonderful freedom to make one's own decisions. This is why so many Welsh miners in those straggling villages in the valleys were determined that their sons and daughters should become teachers.

In India and Africa the same crucial debate has been endlessly re-enacted. In India, for generations, M.K. Gandhi propagated a village educational philosophy designed to ensure that every child should become self-reliant and self-supporting. But British-style élite schools went on turning out lawyers rather than workers,[1] and even in the 1970s, when the benefits of an outmoded Western-style grammar school education reached the remote northern province of Ladakh, with its harsh climate and hard-won self-sufficiency, the results were the same:

> Children struggle with the *Iliad*, and don't learn how to make shoes from yak hair, or how to build an adobe house. If they learn how to build, it is as an engineer with concrete and steel. If they learn how to make shoes, it is from plastic in a factory. If they learn how to grow barley, it is out of books based on the monocultural system, with no allowance for local diversity. These books have no idea about the conditions at 11,000 feet and the wide variety of barley that has grown there and all the local knowledge of minute differences in soil and climate which the local farmer is in tune with. The practical result is that the educated children cannot survive in the village.[2]

Such one-time empire-building nations as Britain and France have no reason to smile either at Dr Banda's £15 million Kamuzu Academy in Malawi,[3] or at the attempt, at the other end of the ideological range, to introduce the British concept of Rural Studies into Kyambe Primary School in colonial Kenya, in David Mulwa's novel, quoted above, where over the door of the Standard Six Classroom were two boards, one saying 'IN THIS SCHOOL YOU

MUST SPEAK ENGLISH' and another saying 'AVOID VERNACULAR. IT MAKES YOU STUPID'.[4] I myself have spoken to people who recalled having been punished in their friendly local primary school because they had been overheard speaking Welsh in the playground.

In Britain, in spite of the efforts of politicians and professional administrators (themselves mostly the products of the private sector in education) to impose a unified system and a unified curriculum, we have several different traditions of public education, stressing different aspects of local relevance and selective opportunity. For convenience we can see them as English, Scottish and Welsh, but even these national labels conceal a variety of regional and local differences in rural educational policy. A Canadian anthropologist who sought to discover the reasons behind the report of the Robbins Committee on higher education found that, 'Parts of East Anglia have the lowest proportions of youth in selective secondary education, while counties in rural North Wales have the highest proportion in the British Isles.'[5] This must, Professor Synge reckoned, be a matter not just of whether or not secondary education had 'gone comprehensive' but of local attitudes to the role of the school and the functions of the education system.

In Scotland, a parish school system, centuries older than its equivalent in England, as well as the fact that the aristocracy was remote and English-educated, ensured that rural schooling was not dominated by landowners, and 'The very structure of country schools, the lack of any distinction between elementary and academic education, ensured that academic education was open to the rural middle classes and to a few lower-class youths. Because of the high number of university students the country had a self-perpetuating supply of teachers. In 1830 nearly half the parishes had at least one teacher who had spent four years at the university.'[6] Even as rural 'dominies', the teachers understood their pupils.

In Wales, dominated by rural nonconformity in opposition to English landowners and industrialists, popular feeling and popular subscriptions set up not only the original University College of Wales but the first secondary schools. 'In contrast with England, where academic secondary education was the preserve of the grammar schools, in Wales popularly elected bodies were allowed to control academic secondary education and tax for its finance .... The Welsh proved ready to tax themselves for secondary education at twice the rate paid in England.'[7]

The English rural poor, by contrast, their overlords having conquered not only the neighbouring countries but half the globe as well, had to suffer the direct rule of the aristocracy, gentry, squirearchy and their immediate employers, the farmers, who ensured that any education children were offered was kept within very closely prescribed limits. 'John Saville, in his study of rural depopulation in England and Wales between 1851 and 1951, found that the argument that education was "ruining" country children was, in his words, "never absent" from discussion of rural life prior to 1914, and continued after the war .... In Essex it was argued in a local council that sending village children to senior schools in larger places "may tend to give them the *town mind* and divert the most able and energetic from agricultural occupations" ... Quite understandably, there remains indifference and sometimes hostility towards education among working-class people in many parts of the English countryside.'[8]

But among their social superiors it was taken for granted that the function of education was to qualify them for those professions which would enable them to get on and get out, whether or not they would return to rural life. 'Who knows what a year or two's Latin may do for him?' asks Tony Lumpkin's mother in Goldsmith's play *She Stoops to*

Conquer, of 1773, and discussing eighteenth-century private schools in Suffolk, Muriel Clegg remarks that it was '... useless to complain as did the *Annual Register* in 1759 that they tried to turn village girls and tradesmen's daughters into accomplished young ladies, if that was precisely what their fathers were looking for'.[9] The historian Tony Wrigley, in the television series on *This Land of England,* stood in the little Lake District grammar school where Wordsworth had been a pupil and described how it had been, for the poet, as for all the local boys who went there, 'an escape route to the world beyond'.[10] To this day parental decisions in farming families depend on elaborate calculations relating to customs of inheritance. It is not uncommon for them to send their boys away to boarding schools and their girls to the local comprehensive, or to make the opposite differential decision. There are places in the British Isles where farmers want a minimal education for their sons, to ensure that they stay on the farm, but the best possible education for their daughters, so that they marry 'off' and 'out'.

The standard history of the education of the country child presents a progression from dame schools in back kitchens, through the efforts of the 'National' and 'British' schools, funded by the churches and chapels respectively, to the work of the School Boards after 1870 and the county councils that superseded them. To this day such mysterious initials as 'VA' and 'VC' remain in the official name of the village school to indicate that it is a 'voluntary' school, either aided or controlled by the local education authority.

The true history is more complex. A centenary publication from the National Union of Teachers explained that, 'Apart from religious and charitable schools, "dame" or common schools were operated by the private enterprise of people who were often barely literate', and it found a reason for the widespread hostility to the school boards with the explanation that, 'Parents were not always quick to appreciate the advantage of full-time schooling against the loss of extra wages.'[11] In the country, the opposition was more frequently from the child's potential employers and from children themselves, anxious to contribute their mite to the family income. Recent historians have, with a mass of statistical evidence re-written the accepted view of the education of the poor.[12]

This is not a completely academic issue, for a county council's decision to close a school includes the asset of the sale of the site and building for conversion into a house at today's prices. Sometimes they find to their embarrassment that the place belongs not to the education authority, nor to the church, but to the anonymous villagers of a century-and-a-half ago who put together their pennies to provide it.

The rural clergy were often, without regard to the National Society for the Education of the Poor in Accordance with the Principles of the Established Church, providers of education for village children, in opposition to the entrenched suspicion from their farmer neighbours.[13]

Ronald Blythe, commenting on the evolution of the village school notes that, 'There were many more village schools before the 1870s than is now popularly supposed, some of them offering eccentric and very interesting curricula as charitable squire or loving clergyman brought in a graduate to give the parish children simple versions of the kind of education they'd had themselves .... Many of these schools were not housed in special buildings but in corners of the church, the vicarage, etc. Bewick was allowed to practice drawing by chalking pictures all over the church floor; and fragments of such education in the form of sand-tables, inkwells fitted to pews and alphabets and multiplication tables painted on vestry walls are still to be found all over Britain.'[14]

But within properly established parish schools, as in Scotland, the majority of pupils were bored to distraction by a curriculum thought appropriate for the academic few. Thus the Commissioners for the Argyll Report of 1867 found that, 'In those old-fashioned parish schools which we visited we found, not infrequently, a class of three or four boys in Latin, two of them, perhaps, the minister's sons and one the teacher's, about a fourth of the school able to read well and write well in copy books, and do a little arithmetic, but the other three fourths unable to spell, or do the simplest sums in arithmetic, and only able to read indifferently. It is quite possible that those three or four boys might go on to the university, but what becomes of the rest of the school?'[15]

This question has preoccupied those who think seriously about the education of the country child for generations. They have been concerned, not like those nineteenth-century farmers, with what minimum of schooling would equip boys and girls to be useful farm or domestic servants but with the question of how the once automatic experiences of rural life could be an education in themselves. Educators in a dozen countries have struggled with the problem of fitting this simple and direct approach into the expectations of the education system. It was the ideology of Rousseau's *Emile*, and it was that of the Concord Academy, Massachusetts, run successfully by Henry David Thoreau and his brother John until 1841. One former pupil recalled that, 'It was a peculiar school, there was never a boy flogged or threatened.' Another remembered the field trips: '... a weekly walk in the fields and pastures, or a sail or a row on the river, or a swim in one of the ponds of the township, and there was much instructive talk about the Indians who formerly lived or hunted there', while yet another recalled the survey made of the Fair Haven Hill, to give the boys experience of surveying. Over a century later, a teacher appointed to a high school in the traditionally depressed and under-achieving Southern Appalachian Highlands began to persuade his pupils to investigate and record the skills, poems, songs, recipes and remedies of their own villages, cut off from the mainstream of American affluence. The result was a quarterly journal which aroused so much interest that it grew into the series of *Foxfire* volumes sold all over the world, produced by the students of the Rabun Gap-Nacoochee School, Georgia.[16]

One of the most telling of such tales of teachers turning disadvantages into valued resources comes from pre-war Germany. Adolf Reichwein was a civil servant in the Ministry of Education in Berlin. When the Nazis came to power, he asked to be sent back to the classroom in a poor country school in a sandy forest in Brandenburg. 'It had about the lowest record for pupils going on the further education in Germany. It had one large classroom only. He, his wife and three children lived in a tiny flat above, with a salary of £350 a year. His allowance for school books and equipment was £5 a year, and he had about fifty pupils.' A visitor reported that, 'We went into a schoolroom full of cheerfully painted desks and well-made simple chairs. Hanging from the ceiling were gay horizontal wheels supporting lamps to light the classes on a winter evening. In one of the dressers bright pottery was stacked for the school lunches. Everything had been made by the children at the school. When he arrived he went to the forester and persuaded him to take classes in forestry in the open. He went to the blacksmith and the carpenter to get them to take classes in their respective crafts .... His children were taught to help themselves. How our educationalists would have frowned at the time the children spent away from the three Rs.'[17] Adolf Reichwein was eventually shot by the Nazis.

In the British educational climate, the elaborate system of controls by local and central government, as well as the machinery of examinations as the passport for employment, ensures that radical experiments in rural education do not happen. Sir Alec Clegg, the former chief educational officer of the West Riding of Yorkshire, used to tell a significant tale: 'About 100 years ago there was a small boy called Fred and he lived on an island with his father and mother and nearby lived his uncle and aunt. His father kept pigeons and bees and a garden of flowers and vegetables. His uncle was a forester and planted acre after acre of trees in rows. The boy did not go to school; there wasn't a school on the island, but his mother taught him to read and write and encouraged him to draw and paint pictures, she also recited poetry to him and sang to him when he was little ....' Sometimes the family took a trip to the mainland to see York and Malham.

> Then one day a learned educationist visited the island and met the boy and was astonished at his understanding of many things and at the knowledge which he had developed round these things, and the educationist said to himself how wonderful it would be if every child in the land had the learning which this boy has built around simple experiences which he has had with bees, pigeons, flowers, vegetables, forestry and visits to York and Malham. And the learned educationist reasoned thus: 'It is impossible for every child to lead the life that this boy has led and to develop the knowledge which this boy's way of life has given him. But what we can do is to give the children all the knowledge that this boy has without the experiences. First of all we will look at his numerical and mathematical ability which he has gained from reckoning areas from odd shaped bits of land and working out the number of trees they will take ....'

... and so on. Sir Alec went on to explain how the formalization into subject areas of Fred's unconsciously acquired wisdom did not work, and told how, 'In due course a few, a very few indeed, intelligent teachers came to take a cool look at what was happening and they realized that for the vast majority of children the majority of our educational processes add about as much to the mental stature of our children as a diet of sawdust would add to their physical stature ....'[18]

In the attempt to incorporate this naturally acquired learning into a classroom topic, every effort of the kind Sir Alec described was certainly made. I have before me Book 5 of McDougall's *Rural Arithmetics*, which, it was claimed, should meet the demand in country schools for books '... which, without omitting an adequate treatment of general arithmetic, should yet deal specially with subjects of peculiar interest to dwellers in the country, and particularly to those children whose future occupations are likely to be concerned with agriculture and the great agricultural industries'. I learn from it that in 1907 there were 2,088,932 horses in the United Kingdom.

Dear to the hearts of those who sought to make schooling relevant was gardening. Frederick Hobley, born in 1833, recalled how, 'Attached to the National School there was a very large garden. The Master had an extra large portion of it. The Schoolmistress had a nice piece, and some 12 or 14 of the older and best-behaved schoolboys had a small piece each – about 2 square poles. I had one of these plots – it was 5½ yards wide and 11 yards long, and in it I grew quite a number of useful vegetables for use in my own home. We used to see who could grow the best, and keep his garden the neatest and cleanest ....'[19] Mrs Nellie Hammond remembered the plot she had before leaving school at thirteen in 1913 to go into domestic service: 'Part of the grounds were divided into plots for the boys. Then a piece was cut out and that was allowed for the girls – about half-a-dozen plots – for girls who were specially interested in gardening. These were cultivated during school time as agricultural lessons. They grew their own vegetables and were also allowed to work out of school time if they wanted to.'[20]

Other schools began keeping livestock, which everyone agreed was an immensely valuable occupation for children, and enthusiastic teachers built up a whole curriculum around the school farm idea.[21] But, of course, it failed to win the esteem of the academics, there was little promotion or prestige for the teachers who were devoted to it and, worse still, the garden or the farm became a convenient dumping place for pupils who were dull, troublesome or no good in classroom subjects. Faced with the prospect of being sneered out of existence, teachers like the late Annesley Voysey formed a Rural Studies Association which grew to be the present flourishing National Association for Environmental Education and developed an examination hierarchy in Rural Studies and Rural Science. There are still rural schools which run their own farm, like Brymore School at Cannington in Somerset, Castell Alun High School at Hope, near Wrexham, where the science department took over a smallholding adjoining the school, and Oathall School near Haywards Heath in Sussex. But where I live, in Suffolk, rural studies are phased out (in, for example, Hadleigh and Bury St Edmunds) with the retirement of the teacher in charge. Now that we have abolished the difference between urban and rural education in the worthy interests of equal opportunity and parity of esteem, it is a low-status subject.

Has anything been lost? I remember talking at the time of the raising of the minimum leaving age from fifteen to sixteen to Sean Carson, then Environmental Studies Adviser for Hertfordshire. He was recalling the 1947–8 school year, when the minimum age was raised from fourteen to fifteen and when, at a stroke of the pen, the rural senior schools and senior departments of elementary schools became secondary moderns. 'Things were different then,' he said. 'I was teaching rural studies and had the leavers' class, as we called it, to myself. I used to give them man-sized jobs. We were lucky, of course: the school had a lot of ground and some livestock, and we had arrangements with farmers nearby. I would give one boy complete responsibility for a sow and her litter. We had a badge for pupils who successfully reared a calf. It just couldn't happen nowadays. The authority wouldn't allow it, and farming has changed so much that farmers couldn't collaborate either. Why, sometimes the whole class and I would go off for the day on bicycles. Would we dare do that today? By the end of the year every boy and girl in the class had learned to drive a tractor. Would they let me do that today?'

As he spoke, I began to think of that period as a kind of golden age. But it was not of course. It was the time of whale meat and Herbert Morrison, makeshifts and shortages, just after the war.

'You know,' Sean went on, 'some of those people who were in my class then still write to me, and it is obvious that the last year was a year of growth and achievement for them.' Would it be for their equivalent today?

13   Schools of Freedom

Sixty years ago, the green was so crowded that I couldn't see over the people's heads. At seventeen years of age I opened the school. They gave me the signal and I said, 'With joy and thankfulness I declare this school open to be forever a school of freedom.'

Violet Potter, at the re-enactment of the Burston School Strike,
Stantonbury Campus, Milton Keynes, 1978

The most remarkable challenges to accepted ideas about rural life and rural education have happened deep in the country. In 1914 the children of the Norfolk village of Burston came out on strike in support of their teachers, dismissed because they offended the automatic dominance of the sporting parson and the hierarchy of farmers. In 1924 Henry Morris, director of education for Cambridgeshire, challenged the accepted notions of rural schooling with the idea of the village college. In 1982 a handful of people in Hartland, Devon, set out to show that a tiny village secondary school was preferable for their children to a fifteen-mile-each-way daily bus journey.

Although the Burston school strike was the longest strike in history, since the alternative Strike School built by public subscription remained open until 1939, its story would have dropped out of public memory, even in the locality, but for the account of it by Reg Groves in his history of the farmworkers' union in 1949.[1] Bertram Edwards read the book in 1971 and felt ashamed that having been a member of the National Union of Teachers for over twenty years, he had never even heard of the events at Burston. He took the train to Diss and walked there, following the route taken by Kitty and Tom Higdon when they arrived as village teachers in 1911. He interviewed twenty former pupils and saw the Strike School with its commemorative tablet telling the story: 'Mr T.G. Higdon and Mrs A.K. Higdon were unjustly dismissed from the Council School of this village on the 31st day of March, 1914. This building was erected by public subscription, to protest against the action of the Education Authorities, to provide a free school, to be a centre of Rural Democracy and a memorial to the villagers' fight for freedom.'

Edwards wrote his book on *The Burston School Strike*, published in 1973,[2] and this led to the television programme by surviving pupils, to the television play *The Burston Rebellion*[3] and in 1983 to a revival of annual rallies by the trade union movement on Burston Green. The story of the Strike School has thus re-entered history through the media, though, with immense irony, by 1986 grandchildren and great-grandchildren of the original striking pupils were demonstrating in support of Burston County Primary School, threatened with closure.[4]

The story of the Higdons is a reminder of the absolute deference to the clergy and the farmers that was expected not only of village children but of their teachers too. Tom Higdon was the branch secretary of the Agricultural Labourers' Union – it was a frequent practice for the organizers not to be labourers because of the fear of victimization. He was, like the pioneers of farm-workers' unions, Joseph Arch and George Edwards, a Primitive Methodist lay preacher, and the first of the new rector's grievances against the Higdons was that, like half the villagers, they attended the chapel and not the church. Then, at the parish council elections, Higdon organized the farm labourers to contest the election, something that had never happened before. 'The result was that all the old members of the council except one (who came bottom of the poll) were replaced by labourers or the representatives. Higdon himself came top.'⁵ The result was an astonishing campaign of vilification against the Higdons, leading to their dismissal by the county education authority on the recommendation of the board of managers. Then the children took the affair into their hands. Emily Wilby, one of the pupils, wrote at the time:

We came on strike on April 1st 1914. We came on strike because our governess and master were dismissed from the council school unjustly. The parson got two Barnardo children to say that our governess had caned them and slapped their faces, but we all knew she did not .... Governess did not know we were going on strike. She brought us all some Easter eggs and oranges the last day we were at the council school. Violet Potter brought a paper to school with all our names on it, and all who were going on strike had to put a cross against their name. Out of seventy-two children, sixty-six came out on strike .... The next morning the sixty-six children lined up on the Crossways. We all had cards round our necks and paper trimmings. We marched past the Council school .... Mrs Boulton, the lady at the Post Office, gave us some lemonade and sweets and nuts. She also gave us a large banner and several flags .... Mr Starr, the Attendance Officer, sent our mothers a paper saying if they did not send their children to school they would be summonsed, but our mothers did not care about the papers; some put them on sticks and waved them .... One day a policeman went round to twenty houses with summonses because we had not been to school ... at Court the fine was half-a-crown each .... The next day our mothers thought we might begin school on the Common while it was fine weather. We had school on the Common a little while, then we went into the very cottage that the Barnardo children had lived in for a year and a half. Our mothers lent stools, tables, chairs etc. Mr Ambrose Sandy said we could have his (carpenter's) shop for a strike school. Sam Sandy came and whitewashed it out and mended the windows. He put a ladder up so that we could go upstairs. Our mothers were soon summonsed again .... Our parents did not have to pay a penny of the fine. It was all collected on the Green and in the streets.[6]

The Labour and trade union movements subscribed to the building of the new Strike School, which remained open until Tom Higdon's death at the beginning of the Second World War. He saw the struggle that had been thrust upon the pupils and teachers as epitomizing 'the whole rural problem of the land and the labourer'.

If Burston was battling for rural democracy from below, Henry Morris engaged in it from above. He was a man of humble origins (which he concealed) and aristocratic tastes. Having been a 'temporary gentleman' as an officer in the First World War, he was appointed assistant to the chief education officer of Cambridgeshire in 1921. In the following year the chief died and Morris replaced him. He stayed until 1954, never dreaming of applying for 'better' jobs with larger authorities, spiralling up the hierarchy of educational administration. For Cambridgeshire (which did not then include the city) was a small, poor and backward county educationally, with low wages, antiquated village schools and a falling population.

At Christmas 1924 every county councillor received a beautifully printed pamphlet produced at Morris's own expense by the University Press. It was called *The Village College* and set out his plan for changing the whole nature of rural education, full of resounding phrases.

If rural England is to have the education it needs and the social and recreational life it deserves, more is required than the reorganisation of the elementary school system .... There must be a grouping and co-ordination of all the educational and social agencies which now exist in isolation in the countryside .... The possibility of bringing together all the various educational and social services would find a habitation within the village college .... We must do away with the insulated school. We must associate with education all those activities which go to make the full life. This is as important for the teaching of the young as it is for the teachers themselves .... It is only in a world where education is confined to infants and adolescents that the teacher is inclined to become a pundit or a tyrant.[7]

Morris's memorandum anticipated a whole range of subsequent innovations and policies: the separation of junior and senior schools, the concept of education as a life-long experience, the whole philosophy of community schools and colleges subsequently developed by his disciples in the post-war years. Education was to be the means of rebuilding rural life. He even foresaw that, 'As we may not always remain predominantly an industrial country, it is necessary that the problem of the reconstruction of the village should be dealt with in good time.'[8]

Morris set about cajoling and bullying his county council into adopting his plan, getting additional sums from trusts and charities and persuading influential friends to donate their expertise. Sawston Village College was opened in 1930, followed by Bottisham, Linton and then Impington (designed by Gropius and Maxwell Fry and regarded as a landmark in modern architecture). The person in charge was called the Warden, to symbolize the fact that he or she was not the head of a school but the administrator of a resource for the whole community.

The colleges multiplied in the post-war years, but when Morris's biographer Harry Rée toured Cambridgeshire, he found that many colleges, and many people connected with them, '... have stood still, and in some cases turned their backs on the hopes and ideals of the originator'. It made him reflect that, 'Simply to call a school a village college, or to change the name of a school to community school, is only slightly less effective than to tack a couple of squash courts and a public swimming pool onto an existing school, and to think that community education will result. Nor is it enough to provide an adult tutor to organize evening classes in the school buildings. This makes little impact on the education of children in the school, and equally little on community development outside.'[9]

Times have changed. Harry Rée was alarmed at the halving of the numbers of 'community tutors', for 'The suspicion grows that, although at one time the landowner councillors supported Morris and community education wholeheartedly, the present generation of conservatives look upon community education with strong disfavour, because it is said to promote dangerous political and educational policies.' They have changed in another sense. Morris was an evangelist of high culture and would simply have been shocked at the sight of village punks with multicoloured hair propping up the bar at the weekly disco. Yet it might be that one of the most important current services that some colleges could perform today is to provide a late-night café serving the needs of teenagers, simply as somewhere to meet. One or two of them do just this.

Institutions are not changeless. Morris claimed in 1924 that, 'The village college would not outlive its function, for the main reason that it would not be committed irrevocably to any intellectual or social dogma or to any sectional point of view. Intellectually it might be one of the freest of our English institutions.'

One of the Cambridgeshire village college wardens was Philip Toogood, who then moved to become head of Madeley Court Community School, Telford, resigning in protest against the policy of the local education authority. His conclusion after many years of teaching is that, 'The justification for "school" in its present form no longer exists. There is now no reason to take children into a large inhuman centre for 7 hours a day, 40 weeks a year, to be looked after and institutionalized by kindly teachers – "parent substitutes". We are depriving the community of its youth. There is another way. It is in community education. There is a need now to restore to the local community the children who are being stolen into daily containment in the classroom. We *need* the school-in-the-community.'[10]

Philip Toogood has now found his niche, teaching part-time at a school which has the ambition of becoming a model for education in rural areas, a small school rooted in the community. This is 'the Small School' at Hartland in North Devon.

There have been a number of ventures by rural parents disappointed by the closure of schools to set up their own. In May 1938 the inspectors reported on Michaelstowe School near Camelford, Cornwall: 'This happy little country school is attended by twenty-one children, seven of whom belong to one family. It has a charming homely atmosphere. The headmistress is devoted to her work and the children repay her interest in them as individuals with ready co-operation and eagerness to learn. They evidently enjoy coming to school. The different groups in which ages range from four to thirteen years are managed with resourcefulness that keeps all interested and busily engaged and ensures steady and good progress.'[11] Everybody's mental picture of the village school! But forty years later the authority closed it and put the building up for auction. An unemployed teacher bought the building for £14,000 and, after incredible difficulties over repairs and drainage, re-opened it in 1981. There was an immense local fund-raising activity, but the venture did not survive. Another Cornish initiative of the same kind, Trevoy School near Launceston, has kept alive.

The Small School at Hartland is different from the others. It is a *secondary* school, started in 1983 by Satish Kumar, whose son was leaving the village primary school and would be faced with a daily thirty-mile round trip to the 1,800-pupil Bideford Comprehensive School. (Hartland's secondary school had closed twenty-five years earlier.) Other parents and pupils found Bideford an unattractive proposition too. A disused Methodist chapel was bought by selling shares in the building itself. By 1985 it was reported that,

> In the past two years the Small School has raised a total of £80,000 for repairs, new buildings, equipment and teachers' pay. The fees are £300 a year. This is a lot for parents who are mostly agricultural workers, but payments can be made in kind – by providing food for the school meals, for example, or fuel for heating, or by providing help of some practical kind. Unemployed parents can send their children free. The community is not an affluent one, but evidently a number of parents found paying for the unknown quantity of the Small School an attractive alternative to the free but distant and impersonal comprehensive. The school started with nine pupils, which was about half the number of leavers from the primary school that year. There are now eighteen pupils, and the intake of five years' primary school leavers should bring them to 40 or so.[12]

As I write, there are twenty-five pupils, aged from eleven to sixteen. The school is not meant to evolve into an independent fee-paying school. It is being monitored by Exeter University Department of Education with the aim of becoming adopted by the county council. The head teacher says, 'The starting point for the Small School is the children and their parents. We do not really choose them. They choose us. We have said that we will take any child who lives in Hartland and refuse others only on the ground of distance. Of course space may soon be a problem but still geographical criteria will prevail. They will have to if we intend to be seen as the secondary school of the village. The curriculum grows out of the needs of the children and the concerns of their parents.'[13]

What links the Burston Strike School, the concept of the Village College and the Small School of Hartland is the belief that rural education can be a creative adventure rather than an administrative headache.

Changing
Childhood

14 Worlds Outside

When I was working in Guatemala City, I was at first surprised to find the quantity of animals that was kept, even in the densely inhabited squatter settlements; chickens and even pigs were a common sight. Indeed, one of my informants criticized a government project to relocate the squatter settlements on the grounds that it would not work since there would be no place for the families to raise their animals.

Bryan Roberts, *Cities of Peasants*, 1978

American sociologists have evolved a 'gradient theory' of the differences between urban and rural life, suggesting that, 'The extent of urban influence in the outlying hinterland varies inversely with distance to the nearest city, and directly with the size of that city.'[1] It is a reminder that in small countries like Britain measurable differences between town and country life have been all but eliminated, geographical distances having been leapfrogged by communications. 'In only one generation, asphalted roads and motorways, electricity cables and telephone lines have eliminated differences in economic potential and living standard between town and country, which still represented a vast gulf in Western Europe down to the 1950s.'[2] Even in countries with a huge land mass like the United States, 'The differentials are undoubtedly converging as a result of increasing accessibility.'[3] No doubt urban American children would instantly recognize a 'hick' or a 'hayseed' in their midst, but they all wear the same clothes, play the same games and watch the same television programmes.

In the other vast nation of the northern hemisphere, the Soviet Union, urban and rural differences are instantly visible.

Follow the country folk toward home at night, in the railroad stations, and you see what Russians call the *narod*, the masses, of whom officialdom and intellectuals privately speak with condescension and contempt. They are coarse, raw, simple people, weatherbeaten as the log cabins in which they live [wrote Hedrick Smith in 1975, watching them at the Kazan station in Moscow]. Follow the *narod* into the countryside and the modern world peels away with astonishing suddenness. Not only the peasantry but the countryside presses in close around Moscow. It surprised me to see that just ten miles from the Kremlin, near the village of Little Mytishchi, city life and its modern conveniences simply come to an end. New apartment buildings give way to *izbas*, squat, low peasant log cabins. Side roads are suddenly no longer paved but turn to dirt .... Thanks to Lenin's belief in electricity, most peasant homes have lights – and television ... [but] By any measure of living standards – income, schools, social life, welfare, health care, consumer goods, leisure outlets, transportation – rural people are worse off than city residents ...[4]

He reflects that it is as if modern civilization '... radiated outward from the cities in concentric circles and the further out, the fewer amenities, the harder the life'.

But this has been true throughout history, and is true today for the greater part of the world. In many of the countries of Africa, Latin America and Asia, the gap between city and country life has widened. Since the 1940s there has been an incredible migration from the country to the city. For millions of people this must be the most important and dramatic event of the twentieth century. And however desperate life may be in the vast shanty towns and squatter settlements, people have made a rational choice between hunger in the city and starvation in the country. 'Much of the increased city population lives in the shanty towns. In the 1960s these contained a quarter of the population of such cities as Manila and Djakarta, a third of that of Mexico City and a half of that of Ankara and Lima. These proportions are furthermore growing; while the rate of city growth is frequently twice that of natural increase, in some states the shanty towns are growing at rates above 10 per cent, that is at double the growth rate of the city. It has been estimated that by 1990 three quarters of Lima's population will be living in shanty towns.'[5]

The World Health Organization calculates that in the northern hemisphere the increase in city population will be from 8 to 11 hundred million, while in the southern half of the world it will be from 8 to 20 hundred million.[6] But this calculation, while dramatizing both population growth and migration, ignores the difficult issue of defining the city. In the north, inner city populations have been declining all through the century: the growth is on the periphery of the city region. In the south, the rate of increase in the city centre is much lower than that in the hinterland.

I used to illustrate for children the pattern of family movement with two true stories, the first told me by the anthropologist William Mangin and the second by James Byrne, a retired carpenter.

Blas Quispe's father, Fortunado, was a Quechua-speaking Indian, a landless labourer on a *hacienda* in the mountain district of Paucartambo in Peru. Fortunado Quispe found it increasingly hard to feed his seven children, so he sought work on a sugar plantation on the coast, and the family moved to a two-room *adobe* hut there. But the plantation was mechanizing and by the time the eldest son, Blas, was eighteen and due for a man's wage, he was told to move on. Like thousands of others, he decided to seek his fortune in Lima, got a lift on a lorry to the edge of the valley where the city stands and took a bus to the city centre. There, as his father had suggested, he sought out the secretary of a club called 'The Sons of Paucartambo', who found him a share of a room and a job in a hotel, where he got no pay, only tips. There he met Carmen, who worked as a maid in the house next door and had come to the city from the southern highland province of Ayucucho. They rented a room together, sharing a tap with ten other families, and decided, having quickly acquired urban know-how, to join a squatters' association.

At dawn on a public holiday they took a taxi, loaded it with their belongings, their children, poles and straw mats and drove to the new *barriada*, pegged out a plot 16 by 33 yards, and built a wall of mats around it. Next morning the police pulled it down. So they built it again, and in the end the police stopped coming back. With the help of friends they replaced the mats with a wall of concrete blocks, strong enough to support a floor above. Gradually Blas, Carmen and their neighbours built a sewer and put in water pipes and wired up the house for electricity, which they bought from another squatter who ran a diesel generator. Then they started to build a school. A few years and several children later, Blas built an upper floor. By now it was becoming something like a fully serviced house. Carmen ran a shop in the front room, and they planned to open a café.

Fifty years earlier Thomas Byrne, at eighteen, left his father's poor little farm in Kerry, in the west of Ireland, and sought work in the city of Cork. Then he moved to Canning Town in London, and his uncle got him a job in the Royal Albert Dock. He married and rented a room in Freemason's Road, where his son James was born. One day the Byrne family took a free excursion train to Laindon in Essex, where an estate agent was auctioning plots of derelict farm land. When they tumbled out of the return train that night, they had bought for a £1 deposit, a £6 plot of land, 6½ yards wide and 33 yards deep, in New Century Road (which was simply a row of pegs in a field). They had their first ever holidays there in an army surplus bell-tent, and planted roses and apple trees from Woolworth's. They built a cabin there and, bombed out in London in the Second World War, moved in for good. James Byrne slowly rebuilt the cabin as a house, and his own children grew up there.

'Were they town children or country children?' he asked me. He and his wife moved further into rural Essex. 'What *I* reckon,' he said, 'is that my family have been country folk, city dwellers, suburbanites and country folk again, all in two generations, and there are thousands like us.'

Naturally I was selecting 'good luck' stories to illustrate patterns of family migration, both in Britain's recent history and in half the world today, and ignoring the millions trapped in urban poverty in the same way as their parents were trapped in rural poverty. But every migrant parent would answer that they moved for the sake of their children. Their assessment of the situation is right.

'In almost all countries, children living in the towns have a lower mortality rate. This is largely related to better education of the mother and socio-economic advantages. One important advantage for children is a steady supply of food. Apparently sewage disposal, water supply and health facilities cannot be shown to play much part. The expensive urban infrastructures do not cause a large reduction in child mortality.'[7]

This is the view of David Morley and Hermione Lovel of the Institute of Child Health in London, and they stress that in every country of the south there is a built-in urban bias. The political and governing élite are in the cities, money is spent on fully equipped Western-style hospitals, not village clinics, and on universities, not village schools.[8]

Jon Bennett makes the same point forcibly: 'Most governments give city people preference, and makes sure they have access to soup-kitchens or food-ration shops .... This is because the governments themselves want to survive: history has shown over and over that urban people get very upset when food is in short supply, and can easily turn into revolutionary mobs! Rural people, on the other hand, are usually dispersed and poorly organized .... In all the pictures of famines we've seen over the past several years, not one has shown a Third World army officer, or cabinet minister or rich shopkeeper starving to death!'[9]

The failure of the rulers of the countries of the poor world to institute effective land reform, their encouragement of cash crops for export rather than subsistence crops for local consumption, and above all their encouragement of multinational agribusiness, pushing peasants off the land, all guarantee that for the sake of their children peasants will migrate to the cities. Some people see this simply as the export of poverty: 'The prosperity of cities such as Cairo, Bombay or Djakarta depends on cheap labour drawn from the rural poor.'[10] Others see it as the 'ruralization' of the city, happening in the south just as the urbanization of rural life is taking place in the north: 'In the shanty towns – which for many purposes are more like country villages re-erected on a scrap of urban wasteland – children are an asset. They start work early, often at five or six years old. They help their parents and relations with the poultry-raising and the vegetable-growing that goes on amidst all the stench and chaos, on the tiny plots occupied by the cardboard and corrugated iron houses.'[11]

Bryan Roberts, in his study of cities of peasants, notes how the boundaries between city and countryside are much less clear than statistical surveys tend to show. Small-scale agriculture '... continues as a supplement to urban work. The lots on the periphery of these cities are sufficiently large to allow some animals to be kept, vegetables and fruit to be grown; the shack houses a family in which several members journey to work in the city leaving others (perhaps an elderly relative or a young child) to cultivate the plot .... In Stanleyville, in the then Belgian Congo, the housing of low-income urban workers was often located in compounds which permitted animals to be raised and crops to be grown.'[12]

In spite of the enormous movements of population, most of the world's people, and consequently most children, are country-dwellers. They are measurably poorer than most urban residents, and these differences are widening. And by now, these armies of the children of poor peasants, share-croppers and landless labourers realize that the millions of urban poor, including the millions of 'street children', have more hope for the future than they do. As Jon Bennett pungently puts it, 'The World Bank has been saying for years that 90 per cent of the world's hungry people live in the countryside. This may change as migration to cities picks up speed, but it is paradoxical that those who produce food, or who could be producing food, are the first to suffer from the lack of it.'[13] Many governments have embarked on programmes of rural development: China, India, Mexico, Cuba, Tanzania and Egypt, but until country people are sure that they are better assured of the means of life than they would be on the fringe of the cities, they will continue to migrate, just as they were obliged to in nineteenth-century Britain.

One of the most interesting and telling studies of all, about the lives of children in the self-built shanty towns of poor Latin American cities, was that directed by the late Kevin Lynch (author of *The Image of the City*). He was invited to examine the opinions of children aged eleven to fourteen in several of the world's cities. They included two contrasting neighbourhoods of Warsaw and Cracow, a western suburb of Melbourne, Australia, a dweller-built settlement called Ecatepec on the northern fringe of Mexico City, and a similar place called Villas Las Rosas on the fringe of the Argentine city of Salta.

The last two places had the happiest children, despite the fact that the boys and girls of Ecatepec were the poorest children in the survey. To the adult investigators the place seemed harsh, bleak and monotonous, and they were puzzled by the affection for this settlement of displaced rural migrants displayed in the children's interviews, maps and drawings. Life for them was visibly improving – 'There is less dust now, houses that used to be shanties are fully constructed, one does not have to go outside the *colonia* for certain services.' They '... consistently named their school as a favourite place, and gave it a loving emphasis on their maps', and the suggestions they made to the interviewers '... reflect a genuine concern for their families, as well as their own future, and an empathy for fellow residents of the *colonia*'.

It was the same at Las Rosas, which to the outsider seemed a place of houses 'put down according to a rather haphazard plan on an old garbage dump next to the penitentiary', but its children repeatedly volunteered the view that Las Rosas was 'nice', friendly, protected and 'fun'. They were convinced that it was changing for the better and expected to live there when they grew up (unlike the wealthiest and best-fed children in the survey, who all wanted to get away from their Melbourne suburb).

At Las Rosas, 'On the hill, the neighbours' association is building a swimming pool, and one or two of the boys helped clear the land for it. They await its completion eagerly but impatiently, since progress is slow .... The Las Rosas yards are full of house extensions, chicken yards, work areas and vine-covered dining places .... Las Rosas has the appearance of a hopeful and active community, however meagre its means. Children play a small but recognizable part in community action.'[14]

This is a remarkable testimony to the qualities that make a childhood environment a good place to grow up in.

15   Trapped Teenagers

They go through an absolutely barren social period in their life before they qualify for the weekly 'car-load' heading for the dance hall in the nearest big town. This is fast becoming the exclusive social pastime in rural parishes for teenage boys and girls.

Maurice Kennedy, *Opportunity for Rural Youth*, 1960

For younger children up to the age of 14, many of their needs are being met, but at a high cost in terms of travelling and time. In the summer young people, regardless of their age, are less likely to be at a loss for something to do, but in the winter the situation is sometimes desperate for many older adolescents. The feeling of depression and the sense of isolation can be seen quite clearly on the faces of many youngsters: lonely people living in one of the most beautiful parts of the country. For many it is nothing more than a social desert.

Allan Kennedy, *Shadows of Adolescence*, 1984

There comes an age when many children who live far from big metropolitan centres yearn to break out of their social desert, overwhelmingly conscious that they have outgrown the narrow range of contacts and opportunities that the all-too-familiar local environment provides. Disapproving parents looking for a scapegoat blame television and the media-promoted youth culture, just as they once blamed cinema and radio, but it has always been like this. That is why boys ran away to sea, and apprentices became, literally, journeymen, and why girls were thrilled when, having been 'broken in' to domestic service locally, they were qualified for a job far from home, packed their trunk and went.

Soon after radio, then called 'the wireless', first

penetrated rural life, the writer C. Delisle Burns gave a series of broadcast talks called *Leisure in the Modern World* which were published together with a fascinating selection of the listeners' letters they provoked. He had mentioned the frustrations of rural life, and 'an interested youth in the country' wrote to say that, 'The fault lies, I think, not in the youth themselves, but in the very nature of their environment. Things move more slowly in a country place. There is not much to talk about and as people must talk, what is more interesting to gossip over than who so-and-so was seen talking to, who so-and-so danced with? Heads begin to nod and tongues to wag, which may be quite harmless, no doubt, but frightfully depressing when one has to live amongst it ....' He compared the range of encounters available in the city with '... the stiff narrow little meetings of the country church social union (sometimes the only public function), where everyone present knows the history of every other from birth .... The town spells "escape" to youth, natural freedom and equality. The country jogs along, thirty years behind the times ....'[1]

Fifty years before that country boy confided his sense of frustration to the BBC in 1932, the novelist Theodore Dreiser was a boy in Sullivan, Indiana. When his elder brother came home from Chicago, he brought back tales of city life: 'You never saw such a place! ... That's the place for a family, where they can do something and get along! Not stuck in a little hole like this! Why, say, there must be four or five hundred thousand people there! And the shops! And the high buildings!' Dreiser himself became similarly intoxicated, not by his eventual move to Chicago, but simply to the 'tiny city' of Evansville, Indiana, which evoked the same exclamation marks, 'Those poor scum back in Sullivan, I thought! What could they know of a place like this? A city! and such a city!'[2]

In the 1960s Susan Hale studied the working and

leisure lives of 120 school-leaver teenagers in rural Herefordshire and remarked that, 'Hanging about on street corners, a reproving phrase one met so often a generation ago, was unknown among our respondents because there were no streets with corners to hang about on. The nearest we come to it is the desultory cycling round and round the war memorial, something that can be seen in most villages on a summer's evening.'[3]

In the 1970s the sociologist Stanley Cohen described the 'edge of desperation' among the young people congregating in the centres of small provincial towns.[4]

In the 1980s Allan Kennedy, a detached youth and community education worker, interviewed young people in West Dorset. What emerges, he says, '... is an image of isolation and depression, of young people experiencing little more than shadows of adolescence'.[5]

But what the surveys actually reveal is not so much a rejection of living in the country as an intense yearning for personal mobility, not only for leisure but also for access to work and to further education. Susan Hale found that out of her 120 Herefordshire sixteen-year-olds,

Asked *where* they want to work, there were less than ten respondents in the whole group who wanted to live and work in a large town ... their attitude can be summed up in the answer of one boy to the question 'Would you like to leave Herefordshire?' 'No why should I?' ... At North School forty out of forty-one children plumped for the country. 'I suppose there's coffee bars and cinemas and that – but I don't care about them'. To most of the respondents 'town' meant Leominster or Ludlow or at the most Hereford. One or two (who had never been there) had a sort of love-hate relationship with London. One boy had spent a week in Birmingham, 'and was I glad to get back?' ... Some (mostly girls) rather grudgingly admitted that they 'wouldn't mind living on the outskirts of a town' but 'People aren't friendly in towns, they don't talk to their neighbours. Look at all those old ladies dying with milk bottles outside their doors!' This aversion to town life did not mean that the respondents were averse to travelling, *quite the opposite.*[6]

Similarly Allan Kennedy in Dorset reported that, 'Of the young people I spoke to, 90 per cent expressed a desire to stay in the area. Very few actually wanted to leave. However, at least a third of those wanting to stay reckoned it was inevitable that they would have to leave at some time in order to find work or start and develop a career of some sort.'[7]

When the parental generation move in search of work but keep rural contacts, their children often hanker for the place of origin. Thus from a forlorn housing estate in the West Midlands, 'Fifteen year old Dan, who had lived all his life on the estate but whose parents took him back to Ireland every summer wrote poignantly, "I belong to Kerry in Ireland no such thing as concrete jungles like this dump. I have spent part of life living on farm surrounded by villages, mountains, seaside. Riding my bike without the risk of being nicked, it's beautiful in County Kerry" ....'[8]

A Shropshire head teacher gave me her explanation of what at first sight seems a paradox. In the past, she said, the big city *was* an irresistible magnet, and those with the opportunity left home. But just because today's children are familiar with the sights and sounds of the city, they are also familiar with its problems, ventilated every day on television. So they get an exaggerated view of the horrors of city life: a mugger on every corner, drug-pushers on every street, and the young, single homeless, ripe for exploitation. 'Except for certain boys and girls, the city has lost its glamour.' On the other hand they yearn for personal mobility, and absolute necessity for jobs, for job training at every level and for social life with others of the same generation. 'Having their own transport is the aspiration of most young people. Even before they are old enough to ride them on the public roads, motor bikes prove to be an irresistible attraction – for girls as well as boys – and owning a car is the ultimate ambition, even if it is 20 years old …. L-plates up at the earliest opportunity! Once the motor bike – even if it is only 125cc – is on the road, it brings a marked increase in independence. But bikes, tax, insurance, maintenance and petrol are costly items …."[9] Above a certain family income level, this of course presents no problems, though sometimes ignorance of the resources that *are* available – motor-vehicle maintenance courses for the amateur, or training courses, assuming that there is a way of reaching them – is an extra impediment. Thus, in his study of the special problems of unemployment in rural Leicestershire, Simon Nicholson mentions how, 'A school leaver wanted a motor-bike, but his parents were worried about safety. He wished to find out about motor-bike training. Information was not to hand but was later provided about the Star Riders scheme in Market Harborough.'[10]

Of course, many secondary schools have a motor-vehicle course, and every rural district has its informal network, mostly of boys, who share problems in keeping 'old bangers' on the road, often with someone working at a garage and attending a motor-vehicle maintenance course at the technical college at its centre. 'Getting it through the MOT' is a constant topic of conversation, and the really skilled improviser and cannibalizer of spares who knows his way around the old car dumps is a very popular person.

But many other country teenagers are really trapped by the tyranny of distance. Susan Hale's study of rural students at Hereford Technical College or working in Hereford City showed this graphically:

Two and a half miles walk home each evening from the next village because the evening bus went an alternative route. This along a busy main road with no footpath (typist).

Four miles bike ride daily along an unmade-up track. 'Spend half my time mending punctures' (plumber apprentice).

Has to walk over fields (half a mile) flooded in winter to reach bus route. Leaves wellingtons in hedge (typist).

Both parents commute daily to work in Hereford City and say they always have 'the car full of youngsters'.

Very isolated farm. Respondent has her own scooter to get to work but parents very anxious about her using it in snow and frost (shop assistant).

Leaves home at 7 a.m., walks one and a half miles to bus. Changes bus and waits twenty minutes for connection, same in evening. Actual mileage covered about thirty-six miles, daily travelling time over four hours (catering student).[11]

She had a host of similar case histories. So do Simon Nicholson from Leicestershire and Allan Kennedy from Dorset:

One 14 year old girl living in Thorncombe was quite happy with her social life, thanks to her parents. They took her to the Youth Orchestra, to the cinema quite regularly, to school discos and on Saturday shopping trips. And while she recognized that she was extremely lucky in having co-operative parents who could afford the time and expense to undertake such journeys, she was still unhappy with some things. 'I'd really like to live in a town. It's all there then – you don't have to travel miles to do things. Mum and Dad take me out a lot but I can't nip round the corner and see my friends when I want to. They're dotted all over the place. I can only see them at school, unless it's a special occasion or something.'

A seventeen-year-old boy told him: 'I managed to get a job as an apprentice electrician and I go to Weymouth Tech once a week. Before I got the motor bike it was terrible. Sometimes I'd get a lift from a friend but once or twice he never turned up so I missed going. Catching the bus means getting up really early and not getting back until late. It's expensive as well, although I do get some of that paid for. When the weather's fine I can go on my bike, but I don't enjoy going in bad weather. It's twenty miles and by the time I get there I'm really knackered.'[12]

Parental income and the consequent accessibility of private transport are the key factors, as well as the ability of teenagers to earn money in their spare time locally. There is everywhere a proportion of teenagers from farm families who, from inclination as well as family expectations, work on the parental holding. It varies according to the locality, whether a pattern of small-scale animal husbandry or of smallholdings survives. And according to temperament: these children can be happy and contented or smoulderingly resentful that they are trapped by circumstance into long hours of work and a low income. The greater proportion of young full-time farm workers come from farming families, were brought up on a farm, were always interested in farming and were uninfluenced by careers guidance at school or from youth employment officers. The most usual reasons for liking farm work are working in the open and working with animals. The commonest reason for eventually leaving it is the low pay, and the usual alternative is road transport, when work is available, because of the better pay.[13]

In the early 1980s, as the crisis of youth unemployment grew devastatingly in the cities, I looked around the Suffolk hamlet where I live, where there were only five people in the sixteen-to-nineteen age range.

Of these, Nigel, a pupil at an independent school in the nearest big town was clocking up the right A-levels to gain admission to a veterinary college (where the demands are even more exacting than those of medical schools).

Katey had just left school and was working in a restaurant in a nearby tourist village, aiming to get onto a catering course.

Ruth went on a pre-nursing course at the county

college, thinking about becoming a children's nurse or a doctor's receptionist. Offered a YOP place in the office of a seed warehouse, she took it and, being pleasant and efficient, was asked to stay on. Not the job she had thought about, but she was happy there.

Nick despised school and was a changed boy once he left. He was, for a change, cheerfully up in the morning on a series of casual jobs – painting the pub, barrowing earth around on a building site – and then got a summer job with a farmer. He yearned to become a gamekeeper.

Barry was the happiest of them all. He left school at the earliest opportunity and slid into work with none of the traumas that sometimes accompany this transition. At sixteen he became self-employed, using an accountant to keep the books and getting his insurance stamps by banker's order. He worked mostly for a small builder in another village, picking up the rudiments of most of the construction trades, without benefit of apprenticeship or a course at the college. It was not his ideal, either. He would rather work on the land, but East Anglian farmers seldom take on workers other than family nowadays, preferring to employ contracting firms at key seasons. Nor do country builders. The man Barry worked for would never dream of doing so, because he could not guarantee the flow of work. Barry joined the growing pattern of self-employment and found it easier to do so because his parents belong in that minority too. They deliver the newspapers, not from a shop but from home, and they also breed pigs and have a field of sugarbeet, belonging to a family network of similar minute enterprises. So his home background made self-employment a natural option as well as a necessity for him.

Most urban children never think about such an option, because nothing, not even careers advisers, has prepared them for it.

Four years later, it is as though these young people had each an inner gyroscope propelling them through life.

Nigel is not going to be a vet but is well into his medical training hundreds of miles away. Katey is college-trained, working in catering. Ruth, experienced and competent, has outgrown her job and is hoping to move. Nick is still 'bumming around', as he puts it, having travelled Europe in a variety of casual agricultural jobs. Barry is well established, experienced and resourceful. The induction into adult life would not have been so smooth and painless for most urban children.

Two of the five are still living at home, and no doubt will do so until they marry or move away. The rest are living or lodging away from home but are still 'home-based'. Their dilemmas, in an area where house prices rise continually while housing for rent diminishes, will begin when they try to enter the market for homes of their own.

16   Styles of Deprivation

When I first taught in a village school, children knew the names and tastes of vegetables their families grew, the difference between hay and straw, a blackbird and a crow. Recently I found only two children between seven and eleven who had ever seen red, black and white currants; none had seen loganberries. They know of bean sprouts and hot rod races. Many pre-school children I met had not seen a vegetable or flower garden, a train, a cow, a market or the inside of any building larger than a supermarket.

Gwen Dunn, *The Box in the Corner*, 1977

The point that Gwen Dunn is making is not that children have changed but that adult habits have changed. She is not blaming television; she is drawing attention to what Kevin Lynch called 'experiential starvation'. This is not an aspect solely of rural isolation. A survey conducted for the Community Relations Commission found that just under half the children under five in the Handsworth district of Birmingham *never* went out to play, and describing an infants' school in Islington in North London, Sue Cameron remarked that, 'The experience of many of these children during the first five years of their lives has been so limited that they come to school like so many blank pages. Near the school is a park and a busy Underground station, but many of the children have never been inside the park and some of them don't know what a tube train looks like.'[1]

But rural deprivation is certainly to be found. Eddie Double of Lincolnshire education department, talked of '… the deprivation that is related to little rows of isolated squalid houses set in the middle of the country. It is the deprivation that comes from the social isolation of children. It is the deprivation that leads to the most massive language and communication difficulties'. Talking of those desolate little Fenland villages, of the kind whose history has been excavated by Mary Chamberlain,[2] he declared that, 'Still today children arrive at school at the age of 4+ or 5, still unable to say more than a few words of their own language. Now this is a real deprivation, this is a real language and communication problem and it is not to be underestimated. It places an enormous responsibility on teachers in rural schools ....'[3]

You can go through the length and breadth of Britain and be told by intelligent and observant people that, 'Nobody's really poor round here any more.' Teachers tell a different story but, seeing more, are less tempted to generalize. Thus Roy Whittaker and Alan Sigsworth, in their sharp little contribution to the debate on rural isolation, where they noted that its alleged effects were exactly the same as those attributed to the inner city environment, draw from real life an example of the way in which circumstances alter cases:

If one attempts to envisage rural isolation at its extreme, then perhaps the picture of a shepherd, his wife and his child living life at the head of a Cumbrian valley might provide a paradigm example. However, even such a simple picture may contain hidden complexities. The shepherd may be an honours graduate who has chosen to tend sheep. His wife may be a teacher who has followed him into the wilderness. Their income, small as it is, may be employed to create a remote yet culturally rich way of living. Their mode of life may be part of a wider pattern involving others with similar values so that, although there are periods of isolation, there may be other periods in which social interaction is intense and demanding for their child.[4]

Whittaker and Sigsworth carefully listed some of the

factors which influence the extent to which isolation implies deprivation, recognizing the diversities of both life styles and life chances. These variable factors include:

a. ownership of the means of accessibility such as cars or telephones …. As income level declines, then not unexpectedly, so does the ownership of cars and telephones; moreover, economic circumstances will powerfully influence the extent to which such means of accessibility can be employed to communicate and range beyond the isolated situation.

b. attitudes to the use of means of access and communication: thus, setting aside economic constraints on use, people will vary in the priority purposes for which they employ cars and telephones; some may employ them predominantly to maintain kinship contacts while others may use them to gain contact with groups and activities beyond the immediate home environment.

c. their composition: one isolated group may be uniformly of the same occupation, religion, political hue and share similar leisure pursuits; another isolated group, although small, may be highly diverse in such features.

d. whether the isolation is chosen or occupationally enforced: in the former case, the conditions of isolation may be consciously manipulated to create a good rearing environment while in the latter, fatalism, or a determination to override circumstance, may profoundly influence the kind of environment in which the child grows up.[5]

This is a very sensitive catalogue of the different styles both of deprivation and of satisfaction in rural areas.

Brian McLaughlin made a study of rural deprivation for the Department of the Environment and the Development Commission which his sponsors have never published. He examined five rural areas in England spread around the country and found that seven per cent of the rural population (nine per cent of households) were living below the DHSS definition of the 'threshold of poverty', as compared with four per cent nationally, that of full-time employees twenty-nine per cent of country-dwellers were defined as 'low paid' as compared with twenty per cent nationally, and that a significant number of earning households in the country '… failed to claim their entitlement in State benefits to assist their finances'.[6] Unemployed people in rural areas are significantly disadvantaged if they are without personal transport or a telephone. The notification of vacancies depends on one or the other, and apart from the fact that the number of public pay-phones in rural areas is declining, the increase in the minimum charge from 5p to 10p in 1984, which was unnoticed by most people, was another inhibition on ringing the Job Centre. Little things like this, and even the cost of the local newspaper, matter when the family budget is minute and when electricity bills and similar recurring expenses are a nightmare.

There is another very disagreeable aspect of rural life at a poverty level. The 'informal economy', opportunities for casual work in agriculture and horticulture, while financial rewards are minimal, has always been important in rural households, but nothing in small communities is private. 'I knew of one unemployed man who did a few hours work on a once-off basis. The DHSS was informed and the individual was brought to book. Yet the same man did extra work before becoming unemployed without anyone informing the Inland Revenue.[7]

Resourceful parents do transcend the limitations of a low cash income to provide a life full of experiences and stimulations for their children. Herefordshire County Council '… defined eight essentials, the absence or inadequacy of which were deemed to denote rural deprivation: water, food shelter/warmth, relationships/communication, health, education, recreation/leisure, and work'. But, comments Malcolm Moseley, 'One need not be a parsimonious county or district councillor to ask whether many rural residents might have opted for a life-style which places a low priority on some of these.'[8] To take an extreme example, a Norwegian study of poor and isolated Lapp families found that many of their attitudes were based on a 'rejection of city ways and a reaffirmation of the rural virtues of independence, tranquillity and morality' and that, in clinging to what their well-wishers saw as an outmoded view of life, 'These groups challenge the very ideological foundation on which the welfare state is built. Rightly or wrongly, these isolated rural groups appear to scorn the attractions of the good, urban life. Although poor, they seem to be about as cheerful as the average city-dweller, and as much attached to their way of life as anybody else.'[9]

You don't have to go to Lapland to find such attitudes. Members of an Amish community in Aylmer, Ontario, Canada, believe that, 'Children nowadays are actually learning less than their parents did in one-room schools', so they run their own, and say, 'Every morning we see the big yellow buses rumble past the end of our lanes. And every morning we are thankful that none of them stop. We consider it a blessing and a privilege to have our children walk to school …. We feel that those who really deserve sympathy are those who not only have to pay for it, but are also trapped into having to use the public schools.'[10] And there are parents, even in semi-suburban Essex, who win the disapproval of the educational industry for the low value they place on schooling and the high value they place on the ability to master skills and machines, to 'pick up a bob or two' and to exploit life's opportunities.

These people have the precious attribute of resourcefulness. Their children make up for the absence of money by the way in which they are to be found at every jumble sale, car-boot event, fair, fête and unofficial market, and ensure that, even if their children's enthusiasms are in expensive activities like rock music, fishing, fashion, horse-riding or trial riding, they belong to the networks through which expensive equipment, materials, electronic gadgetry and animals filter down through the market. The children sleep in each other's houses, borrow each other's clothes and gear and belong to an information network in which one or another has access to the weekly paper with its 'under £35' column, to the advertisements in the newsagent's windows, to the breaker's yard or to the *New Musical Express* or *Exchange and Mart*.

A few of them are actually involved in traditional agricultural pursuits. The children of smallholders are notorious among teachers for their attitude that school is something to be got through quietly while the real business of life is somewhere else. Their dilemma is that they are the kind of child people call an 'old-fashioned' boy or girl. Their family lives are built around production, while the whole culture around them stresses consumption.

Boys in this situation slip automatically into the family business and, as Susan Hale noted many years ago, are often 'either over-protected and spoilt, or exploited'[11] and of course are expected to drive heavy tractors with little understanding of accident precautions. Girls are much worse off. Unless they have broken out into deciding their own future, there are very few occupational ambitions open to them. Hairdressing is one and is a very overcrowded occupation. For some others, of course, the jobs involved in 'horsiculture' (which is a growth industry) are an alternative. But neither of these favoured occupations is likely to be the one for an isolated girl in an isolated place. It is still accepted by them as much as by their parents that they are destined for early marriage and family-raising in, as their mothers firmly hope, more accessible places. Long-established attitudes last longer in the country.

But, allowing for the survival of old attitudes that raise unseen barriers around the expectations of country girls, there is a section of the rural population, just as there is in urban areas, consisting of (as Simon Nicholson lists them) 'the unskilled, the illiterate, the over 50s, those lacking in confidence etc'[12] whose children are disadvantaged because they are often unable to hook themselves onto the networks built up by their better-informed, better-connected but not necessarily better-off peers.

If I had a recipe for alleviating this particular kind of deprivation, I would pass it on. I do know that there are plenty of unskilled, illiterate etc parents who do manage very well to give their children the opportunities they are conscious that they missed themselves. Class assumptions often get in the way. In the same village there are other parents who want to make a success of the pre-school play-group but lack not the willingness but the tact to pick up the children from that track up the hill. Malcolm Moseley is right to perceive that, in our individualistic world, a simple thing like car-sharing, '... runs up against severe socio-cultural problems'.[13]

It was Moseley too, who concluded, like other investigators, that the problem of rural deprivation has always focused on the *consumers* of deprivation rather than on the *producers*. 'In short, academics and planners must no longer imagine that the problems of the rural deprived are best understood by focusing upon the rural deprived – or indeed upon rural regions at all.'[14] This is small comfort either for deprived people or for those who as teachers or as organizers of leisure activities want to mitigate the consequences for children of growing up poor in the country.

I am reminded of a famous dispute in the world of anthropology. Robert Redfield wrote a study of the Mexican village of Tepoztlan, and ten years later Oscar Lewis studied the same village and reached totally different conclusions. Redfield replied with the comment that, 'There are hidden questions behind the two books that have been written about Tepoztlan. The hidden

question behind my book is "What do these people enjoy?"
The hidden question behind Dr Lewis's book is, "What do
these people suffer from?" '[15]

We can ask either of these questions about the isolated
children of the rural poor. What we cannot ignore is that a
little more money in the family budget and a little more
effort in increasing the accessibility of public services
would make a great deal of difference.

17   Country Futures

There is a man I know who farms ten thousand acres with three men (and the use of some contractors). Of course he can only grow one crop, barley, and of course his production per acre is very low and his consumption of imported fertilizer is very high. He burns all his straw, puts no humus on the land and he knows perfectly well his land will suffer in the end. He doesn't care – it will see him out. He is already a millionaire several times over. He is the prime example of that darling of the agricultural economist – the successful agri-businessman …. Cut that land (exhausted as it is) up into a thousand plots of ten acres each, give each plot to a family trained to use it, and within ten years the production coming from it would be enormous …. The motorist wouldn't have the satisfaction of looking out over a vast treeless, hedgeless prairie of indifferent barley – but he could get out of his car and wander through a seemingly huge area of diverse countryside, orchards, young trees plantations, a myriad of small plots of land growing a multiplicity of different crops, farm animals galore and hundreds of happy and healthy children ….
John Seymour, *The Fat of the Land*, 1974

John Seymour's vision of a restoration of the peasantry is often quoted, like Cobbett's outrage at a proposed enclosure 150 years earlier ('Was it a "waste" when a hundred, perhaps, of healthy boys and girls were playing there of a Sunday, instead of creeping about covered in filth in the alleys of a town?[1]). One of the several reasons is precisely because of the persistent feeling that the country is *the* right place in which to rear children.

The historian John Barrell felt obliged to warn us against such dreams that at some time in the future some kind of upheaval will occur, '… whether in the availability of natural resources, the cost of modern farming methods, or simply in the consciousness of city-dwellers, after which, as it were inevitably, large numbers are enabled, or obliged, to return to the land, each family to its ten-acre plot, where they discover the arduous delights of self-sufficiency or community living'. And he 'with little hesitation' makes two predictions: 'The first is that, short of a political revolution, the price and rent of land will not decline in real terms, for land will become no less valuable a commodity than it is now: so that whatever movement back to the land may be necessary to attempt to increase a drastically reduced food supply, it is far more likely to swell the numbers of an impoverished class of small landowners and tenant farmers. The second is that, in so far as the possible futures of this country can be determined by its inhabitants, they will be determined by conflict among those able and willing to organise politically.'[2]

This is a sober warning, but two important points need to be made. The first is that the outward movement of population from British cities has been a feature of the whole history of the century. The garden city pioneer Ebenezer Howard declared in 1904 that, 'While the age in which we live is the age of the great closely-compacted, overcrowded city, there are already signs, for those who can read them, of a coming change so great and so momentous that the twentieth century will be known as the period of the great exodus, the return to the land ....'[3] This was not, of course, the return of Cobbett's cottagers. It was an extension down the social hierarchy of the habit the wealthy had always taken for granted: that of living in the country with access to the town.

In the first forty years of this century, when, in the prolonged agricultural depression, farm land was literally dirt cheap, it did become possible for poor people, with no capital at all, to move out of the city and build their own place in the sun. The places they built, in the Pitsea-Laindon area of Essex or in the weald of Kent or the Hampshire uplands, were despised and deplored by all right-thinking, well-housed people. Anthony King, in his history of the bungalow, explains that, 'A combination of cheap land and transport, pre-fabricated materials, and the owner's labour and skills, had given back to the ordinary people of the land, the opportunity denied to them for over two hundred years, an opportunity which, at the time, was still available to almost half of the world's non-industrialized populations: the freedom for a man to build his own house. It was a freedom that was to be very short-lived.'[4] This actually was a working-class 'back-to-the-land' movement,[5] ended by the post-war planning legislation which was intended to preserve those 'precious agricultural acres'.

Suddenly, in 1987, came the prospect of change in the British application of Common Market policy, which in Britain has favoured the large-scale agricultural businessman but in other EEC countries has been used to protect the interests of the small producer. It is argued that by 1995 there will be a surplus of 700,000 acres of farmland but a continued diminution of the number of people working on the land (0.75 per cent of the full-time working population in 1986, a total of 150,000).[6] Proposals are made for forestry and for an increase in recreational use of this surplus land. Few commentators have urged that underprivileged people, anxious to change the pattern of their lives, should settle in the country, though the director of the Council for the Protection of Rural England, suggested that the time had come for the restoration of the Commons,[7] and the Town and Country Planning Association urged that, 'There may be scope in certain locations to encourage small-holdings of perhaps two to five acres, the income from which would supplement other home-based enterprises.'[8] This is an interesting and realistic acceptance of the fact that, while it is very unlikely that a family could earn a useful income by intensive horticulture on a tiny smallholding, it *could* work in conjunction with other sources of money, as it does for many rural families in Germany, France and Italy.

In the nineteenth century the rural poor had to escape from poverty in the country to the prospect of work in the city. In the twentieth century the affluent have been able to move deep into the country, while the poor, with the same aspirations, have been trapped in the cities whose economic bases have withered away.

People in the world of environmental planning have been watching this for years. In 1972 the planner Roy Gazzard remarked that, 'Cities are becoming the habitat of the have-nots, and the countryside is becoming the habitat of the haves, who are enjoying their life there with people of like interests. Are we going to have a new fascist élite, based on the countryside, with Landrovers, videophones and technological gadgetry, completely independent of the rest of the population?'[9] Ten years later, when Professor Peter Hall came to write the final report of the Social Science Research Council's Inner Cities Working Party, he had to remind us that mistaken prescriptions could result from our stereotypes of the inner city population since, as he put it, 'A majority of inner city people are not poor' and since 'Most of the poor live outside inner cities.'[10]

Allowing for the fact that there is a sense in which we can say that only the rich can afford to live in the country, we can also complain that only the rich can afford to live in the inner city. Since others live there on sufferance or through subsidy, there is also a sense in which we can perfectly well understand what Maurice Ash, chairman of the Town and Country Planning Association, meant when he roundly declared that the combination of attempts to shore up the inner cities amounted in practice to nothing less than a conspiracy to *contain* the disadvantaged: '... a conspiracy', he said, 'because it suits the policies of our centralized state to keep the cities as prisons for the poor.

It suits both those who want to manipulate the poor for reasons of power, and those who want to keep them from the preserves of the rich.'[11]

There is an assumption that the post-war New Towns policy stole both jobs and skilled people from the cities, but the truth is that most new town jobs have been newly generated and would never have gone to the cities, while the importance of the new towns was that they were the one opportunity to move out into rented, rather than freehold, housing. The establishment of Green Belts, with all-party support, has produced what Peter Hall long ago called 'a civilized form of apartheid'. The rich can buy their way into the Green Belt; the commuting middle classes can leapfrog it into new settlements and old country towns and villages beyond it. 'How lovely to own a house in an area – town edge, village or green belt – where competition had been removed. Most of the good people who appear at public enquiries to object to development do not, I think, realize that they are supporting gross and unprincipled greed.'[12]

In the 1970s the Department of the Environment commissioned a series of Inner Area studies, and the one called *Inner London, Policies for Dispersal and Balance* made it clear that, contrary to the conventional wisdom, excessive population pressure in London '... had been unsufficiently relieved by decentralization, either planned or unplanned'.[13] The study confirmed that there *are* poor people in the inner city who *do* want to get out. All the other evidence identifies policies that ensure that they cannot. The avenues of escape have been closed, one by one. Thus it was not at all fatuous for a reader of the reports that filled the press in 1986 about the police pursuit of the 'hippy convoy' around the west of England to comment, 'May I commend the initiative of the "hippies" in removing their children from the urban wastelands .... These people have endeavoured to teach their children self-reliance and to show them the beauties of the countryside. They practise the epitome of Victorian values .... The harassment by the authorities and police; the vilification by the media; and the general nastiness of human nature disgorged upon the poor give the lie to the notion that freedom exists for any but a privileged class .... The saga demonstrates the requirement of a bill of rights for all the citizens of the land.'[14]

Was this an exaggerated response? Not at all, for on one of the few occasions when this group of people were asked for their own opinions, on television,

> Several members interviewed contrasted the convoy way of life explicitly with living in the cities, and described it as a consciously chosen alternative. They feared that the current harassment and impounding of vehicles is likely to leave them with no choice but to go back to the cities. They talked about a difference in quality of life between being unemployed in the city and unemployed in the community of the convoy. They talked about their right to choose the convoy life and not to be forced to live in the city. In choosing *mobile* accommodation, the convoyers are effectively exploiting the *only* remaining loophole (thanks to the traditional rights of bona fide gypsies and holiday caravanners) available to people without cash, mortgage creditworthiness or access to new town rented accommodation who nevertheless are determined to escape the city – a loophole which, as we can see, is currently being mercilessly tightened.[15]

There was a time when desperate solutions like that of becoming mobile ruralists in clapped-out old buses, just to get into the country, would have seemed absurd. But people do make rational choices, from their own standpoint, of the opportunities available to them, and they make them, as do the poor in the Third World flocking *into* the expanding cities, for the sake of their children. The convoyers are the visible, newsworthy tip of an iceberg of popular yearnings.

These popular yearnings correspond to demographic facts. As Peter Hall puts it, 'All over Europe, it almost seems as if we are reverting to the settlement patterns of the middle ages. The rude disturbances of the first industrial revolution, which dragged our ancestors from the fields and into the mines and satanic mills, have been stilled; we return to our roots. The maps of population change in the 1980s are almost the precise inverse of those of the 1880s. But we come back to the land with the aid of the newest technology. It is not the ploughshare and the grist mill that welcome us, but the station wagon and the video recorder.'[16]

Handbooks, both serious and frivolous, are published as guides for the new country-dwellers. Only one of them is addressed to the non-station-wagon, non-range-rover classes.[17] And only one author has tackled the issue of enabling poor people to join this return to rural life. He is Robert Van de Weyer, parish priest and Cambridge economist. His book *Wickwyn: A Vision of the Future* brilliantly encapsulates village history and prophesies a post-industrial rural regeneration. He remarks that, 'Changing economic circumstances have throughout mankind's history caused movements of population. Government policy in the latter half of the 20th century sought to inhibit further spontaneous movement. Planning laws enacted in the 1940s, designed to maintain good order in the use of land, in effect confined the majority of the population to the cities. Wickwyn and numerous villages like it, having declined to tiny hamlets, were not allowed to grow.'[18] And like Peter Hall he does not hesitate to call the result apartheid. He reminds us that almost a quarter of the population of Great Britain now live in jobless families and, as jobs in manufacturing industry and related services continue their steep decline, this figure is set to rise. 'In Britain we have an elaborate system of planning laws and public health regulations which reserve the villages, market towns and leafy suburbs for the privileged members of society with jobs, while the jobless are forced to remain in decaying cities.'[19]

Interviewed about his vision of the future, standing in the real village of Winwick, he explained: 'We ought to make it easy instead of impossible for the city unemployed to come out here, have their own plot of land and build their own houses.' Asked how the existing population would react, 'Oh, they'd hate it of course,' he replied with all the insouciance of a prophet.[20]

They would, but for two separate reasons. The affluent incomers would hate it because they want the village to be historically frozen exactly as it was when they first saw it. Belonging to the mobile élite, it is not important to them whether or not the school or the shop or public transport is viable. The remaining indigenous inhabitants would hate it because, as elsewhere in the country, the houses that used to be cheaply rented are now sold freehold at prices far beyond the reach of either them or their grown children, while virtually no new housing for rent is being built by local authorities. Here the experience of the cities is very relevant for the rural future. Amid the urban gloom of the 1980s we have seen poor urban families, including unemployed people, actually housing themselves through forming housing co-operatives (for example, the Weller Streets Co-op and the Eldonians in the heart of Liverpool, and the Lewisham Self-Build Housing Association in London[21]). They faced immense difficulties from bureaucracy and from the system of housing finance, because their aspirations failed to fit ingrained assumptions about who is entitled to house themselves. Once the artificially inflated value of housing land in the country had been exploded, initiatives like these would be easier there than in the cities.

The complete change in attitudes that this kind of transformation of rural life involves requires such an effort of re-education and political will that it is unlikely to happen unless it is forced upon us by economic crisis and social upheaval. There is no sign at all of the social imagination and political determination to make these changes.

Most people's individual decisions in life are dominated by their hopes for their children. Is the country the ideal child-rearing habitat? This book has tried to penetrate beyond sentimental myths at the advantages and constraints of country childhood. Children do not choose their parents, their economic circumstances or their place of residence. Let's help them make the best of what they've got.

Notes

Introduction and Acknowledgements

1. Susan Isaacs, Clement Brown and R.H. Thouless, *The Cambridge Evacuation Survey* (Methuen, 1941)
2. D.E.M. Gardner, *Susan Isaacs* (Methuen, 1969). A more recent study of her work is Lydia A.H. Smith, *To Understand and to Help: The Life and Work of Susan Isaacs* (Associated University Press, 1985)
3. Brian McLaughlin, 'Rural Rides' in *Poverty*, No. 63, Spring 1986

Chapter 1

1. Raymond Williams, *The Country and the City* (Chatto & Windus, 1973)
2. Emerson's journal quoted by Morton and Lucia White *The Intellectual versus the City* (Mentor Books, 1964)
3. Herbert Read, *The Education of Free Men* (Freedom Press, 1940)
4. P. Williams-Freeman, *The Effect of Town Life on the General Health* (P.S. King, 1890)
5. J. Milner Fothergill, *The Town Dweller: His Needs and Wants* (Longmans, 1889)
6. *Report* of the Inter-Departmental Committee on Physical Deterioration, 1904
7. Mary G. Barnett, *Young Delinquents: A Study of Reformatory and Industrial Schools* (Methuen, 1913)
8. Reginald Bray, *The Town Child* (P.S. King, 1907)
9. Karl Weidel, '*Stadt und Land in Kulturphilosophiscer Beleuchtung*' 1927, quoted in Andrew Lees, *Cities Perceived: Urban Society in European and American Thought 1820–1940* (Manchester University Press, 1985)
10. Leo Tolstoy, 'On Popular Education' (1862) in *Tolstoy on Education* (University of Chicago Press, 1967)

Chapter 2

1. Peter Laslett, *The World We Have Lost* (Methuen, 1965)

2. Mary Russell Mitford, *Our Village*, 1824–32 (George Harrap, 1947)
3. Flora Thompson, *Lark Rise* (Oxford University Press, 1939)
4. Alison Uttley, *The Country Child* (Faber & Faber, 1931)
5. Winifred Foley, *A Child in the Forest* (BBC Publications, 1974)
6. William Godwin, *Enquiry Concerning Political Justice*, 1792 (Penguin Classics, 1976)
7. Pamela Horn, *The Victorian Country Child* (Roundswood Press, 1974)
8. Richard Scase and Robert Goffee, *The Real World of the Small Business Owner* (Croom Helm, 1980)
9. John Burnett (ed.), *Destiny Obscure: Autobiographies of Childhood, Education and Family from the 1820s to the 1920s* (Allen Lane, 1982)
10. James Munson (ed.), *Echoes of the Great War: The Diary of the Rev. Andrew Clark 1914–1919* (Oxford University Press, 1985)
11. J.W. Robertson Scott, *England's Green and Pleasant Land*, 1925 (Penguin, 1947)
12. George Bourne, *Change in the Village*, 1912 (Penguin, 1984)
13. G.F. Seymour in June Jones and Julia Thorogood (eds.), *When I Was a Child* (Ingatestone: Sarsen Publishing for Age Concern (Essex), 1985)

Chapter 3

1. Robin Page *The Decline of an English Village* (Davis-Poynter, 1974)
2. Raymond Williams, *The Country and the City* (Chatto & Windus, 1973)
3. The latest of a succession of studies of the impact of the enclosures is K.D.M. Snell, *Annals of the Labouring Poor: Social Change and Agrarian England 1660–1900* (Cambridge University Press, 1985)
4. Howard Newby, *The Deferential Worker: A Study of Farm Workers in East Anglia* (Allen Lane, 1977)
5. H. Peake, *The English Village: The Origin and Decay of its Community* (Ernest Benn, 1922), quoted in John Connell, *The End of Tradition: Country Life in Central Surrey* (Routledge & Kegan Paul, 1978)
6. William Cobbett, *Rural Rides*, 1830 (Everyman's Library, 1912)
7. Heather E. Hudson, *When Telephones Reach the Village: The role of telecommunications in rural development* (Ablex Publishing, 1985)

8. Geoffrey Barber, *Country Doctor* (Boydell Press, 1970)
9. David St John Thomas, *The Country Station* (David & Charles, 1976)
10. George Bourne, *Change in the Village*, 1912 (Penguin, 1984)
11. John Hibbs *The Country Bus* (David & Charles, 1986)
12. D.P.S., 'Country bus still has a vital part to play in rural life', *East Anglian Daily Times*, 12 April 1986
13. Jeffrey Richards and John M. MacKenzie, *The Railway Station: A Social History* (Oxford University Press, 1986)
14. Anthony Russell, *The Country Parish* (SPCK, 1986)
15. Malcolm J. Moseley, *Accessibility: the rural challenge* (Methuen, 1979), citing M. Brown and S. Winyard, *Low Pay on the Farm* (Low Pay Unit, 1975)
16. Ibid.
17. Howard Newby, *The Deferential Worker* (Allen Lane, 1977)
18. Kenneth Fox, *Metropolitan Communities* (Macmillan, 1985)
19. Nick Bagge in *East Anglian Daily Times*, 4 August 1987
20. Richard Mabey, *In a Green Shade* (Hutchinson, 1983)
21. Gwen Dunn, *The Box in the Corner: Television and the Under-fives* (Macmillan, 1977)

Chapter 4

1. M.F. Ashley Montagu, *The Direction of Human Development: Biological and Social Bases* (Watts, 1957). Dr Jean Itard's own account of *The Wild Boy of Aveyron* is included in Lucien Malson, *Wolf Children* (New Left Books, 1972)
2. A.S. Neill, 'Savagery starts at home', *Anarchy 59*, January 1966
3. Susanna Agnelli, *Street Children, A Growing Urban Tragedy: Report for the Independent Commission on International Humanitarian Issues* (Weidenfeld & Nicolson, 1986)
4. Raynes Minns, *Bombers and Mash: The domestic front 1939–45* (Virago, 1980)
5. A.F. Philp and Noel Timms, *The Problem of the 'Problem Family'* (Family Service Units, 1957)
6. Women's Group on Public Welfare, *Our Towns, a Close-up* (Oxford University Press, 1943)
7. Cited by John Macnicol, 'The evacuation of schoolchildren' in Harold Smith (ed.), *War and Social Change: British Society in the Second World War* (Manchester University Press, 1986)

8. Dorothy Burlingham and Anna Freud, *Young Children in Wartime* (Allen & Unwin, 1942)
9. Susan Isaacs (ed.), *The Cambridge Evacuation Survey: A Wartime Study in Social Welfare and Education* (Methuen, 1941)
10. Barnett House Study Group, *London Children in Wartime Oxford: A Survey of Social and Educational Results of Evacuation* (Oxford University Press, 1947)
11. Susan Isaacs, op. cit.
12. Barnett House Study Group, op. cit.
13. John Macnicol, op. cit.
14. Arthur Marwick, *The Home Front* (Thames & Hudson, 1976). The key works are Richard Titmuss, *Problems of Social Policy* (History of the Second World War, United Kingdom Civil Series, HMSO and Longmans, 1950) and Richard Titmuss, 'War and Social Policy' in his *Essays on 'the Welfare State'* (Allen & Unwin, 1958)
15. It was in fact a repetition of the experience of the First World War described in Pamela Horn's revealing book.
16. John Macnicol, op. cit.
17. 'War memories flood back as evacuees revisit village', *East Anglian Daily Times*, 9 September 1985
18. Susan Isaacs, op. cit.
19. Carlton Jackson, *Who Will Take Our Children: the story of the evacuation in Britain 1939–1945* (Methuen, 1985)
20. Alex Hastie, 'A Love of Country Life' in Robert Westall, *Children of the Blitz: Memories of Wartime Childhood* (Viking, 1985)
21. Gwen Dunn, *The Box in the Corner* (Macmillan, 1977)
22. John Macnicol, op. cit.
23. Carlton Jackson, op. cit. He is quoting a Mass Observation report from Walthamstow in the Tom Harrison Mass Observation Archives at the University of Sussex.

Chapter 5

1. A popular graphical interpretation of these differences, as well as a comprehensive list of statistical sources, is to be found in Stephen Fothergill and Jill Vincent, *The State of the Nation: An Atlas of Britain in the Eighties* (Pan Books, 1985)
2. Anthony Russell, *The Country Parish* (SPCK, 1986)
3. Walter T. Martin, 'Ecological change in a satellite rural area', *American Sociological Review*, Vol. 22, April 1957
4. R.E. Pahl, 'The urban-rural continuum', *Sociologia Ruralis*, Vol.

VI, 1966, reprinted in R.E. Pahl, (ed.), *Readings in Urban Sociology* (Weidenfeld & Nicolson, 1968)

5. F. Barr, 'Urban and Rural Differences in Ability and Attainment', *Educational Research*, Vol. I, No 2, 1959

6. Ibid.

7. *Interim Report on County Reading Survey of May 1975* (Kent County Council, 1977), cited by Roger Watkins, 'Educational Disadvantage in Rural Areas' in M. Shaw (ed.) *Rural Deprivation and Planning* (Geo Books, 1979)

8. Derek Twine, 'Some Effects of the Urbanisation Process on Rural Schoolchildren', *Educational Studies*, Vol. I, No 3, October 1975

9. Ibid.

10. *Basic Education and Teacher Support in Sparsely Populated Areas: England 1978/9* (Centre for Education Research and Innovation and Organisation for Economic and Cultural Development, 1980)

11. Kevin Lynch, *Growing Up in Cities* (MIT Press, 1978) and C. Ward, *The Child in the City* (Architectural Press, 1978), Chapter 5, 'Privacy and Isolation'

12. Council of Europe Symposium on Pre-School Education in Sparsely Populated Areas, *Compensatory Education of Children Living in Socio-Cultural Isolated Areas* (September, 1977)

13. Roy Whittaker and Alan Sigsworth, 'Rural isolation: a cautionary research comment' in *Educational Disadvantage in Rural Areas* (Centre for Information and Advice on Educational Disadvantage, 1980)

14. Ibid.

15. Charles Osborne (ed.), *The Dictionary of Composers* (Bodley Head, 1977)

16. Brian Large, *Martinů* (Duckworth, 1975)

17. Charles Osborne, op. cit.

Chapter 6

1. Christopher Saville, 'Perception of Teachers' In-Service Education Needs in Rural Areas', Tenth International Conference on Rural Education, Keswick Hall, Norfolk, July 1977

2. Quoted in Barbara Wood, *Alias Papa: a life of Fritz Schumacher* (Jonathan Cape, 1984)

3. Denis Pym, *The Employment Question and other essays* (Freedom Press, 1986)

4. Gwen Dunn, *Simon's Last Year: The story of a Suffolk village school*, 1959 (Barbara Hopkinson Books, 1986)

Chapter 7

1. Elsie J. Oxenham, *The Girls of the Hamlet Club* (W. & R. Chambers, 1914)
2. F.G. Thomas, *The Changing Village: An Essay on Rural Reconstruction* (Thomas Nelson, 1939)
3. Malcolm J. Moseley, *Accessibility: the rural challenge* (Methuen, 1979)
4. Anthony Russell, *The Country Parish* (SPCK, 1986)
5. Transport Act, 1968, Section 30
6. Moseley, op. cit.
7. *The Economist*, 16 February 1980
8. *The Conspiracy Against Village Schools*, 1986, prepared by parents from Easton Royal School, Wiltshire, and obtainable for £1 from the National Association for the Support of Small Schools, 91 King Street, Norwich. The study referred to is T.R. Lee, 'On the Relation Between the School Journey and Social and Emotional Adjustment in Rural Infact Children', *British Journal of Educational Psychology*, Vol. 27, 1957
9. Terence Lee, 'Unwittingly to School', *Psychology Today*, Vol. I, No 2, May 1975
10. 'Parents may "ride shotgun" on bus', *East Anglian Daily Times*, 27 June 1987
11. *Ibid.*, reporting meeting of Suffolk County Council's school transport sub-committee
12. Terence Lee, Letter to *The Times*, 5 September 1978
13. *The Conspiracy Against Village Schools*, op. cit.

Chapter 8

1. Yashar Kemal *Memed, My Hawk*, trans. Edouard Roditi (Collins, 1961)
2. Iona and Peter Opie, *Children's Games in Street and Playground* (Oxford University Press, 1969)
3. Henry Williamson, Introduction to the Everyman Edition of *Bevis* (see below)
4. Richard Jefferies, *Bevis, the story of a boy*, 1882 (Everyman's Library, 1981)

NOTES

5. Siegfried Sassoon, *The Old Century, and seven more years* (Faber & Faber, 1938)
6. Ibid.
7. Camilla Campbell, *The Peewit's Cry – a Norfolk Childhood* (East Anglian Magazine Ltd, 1980)
8. Julian Fane, *Morning* (John Murray, 1956)
9. Geoffrey Haslam, *Dens: everyone's architecture for everyone* (unpublished dissertation, Hull School of Architecture, 1982)
10. 'Boys' den drives officials up tree', *Daily Telegraph*, 15 April 1987
11. Marion Shoard, *The Theft of the Countryside* (Temple Smith, 1980)
12. Marion Shoard, *This Land is Our Land: The Struggle for Britain's Countryside* (Paladin, 1987)
13. H. Newby, C. Bell, D. Rose and P. Saunders, *Property, Paternalism and Power: Class and Control in Rural England* (Hutchinson, 1978)

Chapter 9

1. *Education in Rural Wales* (Welsh Department of Education, Pamphlet No. 3, HMSO, 1949)
2. Edward Thomas, *Richard Jefferies, 1909,* (Faber & Faber, 1978)
3. Richard Mabey, *Gilbert White: a biography* (Century, 1986)
4. Gilbert White, *The Natural History of Selborne*, 1788 (Penguin English Classics, 1982)
5. W. Kenneth Richmond, *The Rural School: Its Problems and Prospects* (Alvin Redman, 1953)
6. Fraser Harrison, *The Living Landscape* (Pluto Press, 1986)
7. *Providing for Children's Play in the Countryside* (Countryside Commission for Scotland, 1984)
8. *Talking About Play: A Survey of the Views of Rural Children* (Humberside Playing Fields Association, 1984)
9. Joe Santaniello, 'Rural Deprivation' in *The Country Child* (Lincoln: Centre for the Study of Rural Society, 1978)
10. *Talking About Play*, op. cit. This report is published by Humberside Playing Fields Association, 14 Market Place, Howden, Goole DN14 7BJ.

Chapter 10

1. *Structure Plans and Rural Communities* (National Council of Social Service, 1979)

2. Richard Sennett, *The Uses of Disorder: Personal Identity and City Life* (Penguin, 1971)
3. Colin Ward, 'Making Planning work for People', People and Planning conference, Newcastle Polytechnic, 21 October 1972
4. John Barr, 'Durham's murdered villages', *New Society*, 3 April 1969
5. Jon Gower Davies, *The Evangelistic Bureaucrat* (Tavistock, 1972)
6. Anthony Russell, *The Country Parish* (SPCK, 1986)
7. 'Kersey a dying village, says youth leader', *East Anglian Daily Times*, 19 August 1980
8. Duncan Graham, Chief Education Officer for Suffolk, in *Education*, August 1985
9. Paul Cloke, *Key Settlements in Rural Areas* (Methuen, 1979)
10. Ian Gilder, *Rural Planning Policies: An Economic Appraisal* Progress in Planning, Vol. II, Part 3 (Pergamon, 1979)
11. Ian Gilder, 'Do we need Key Settlement policies?', *The Planner*, Vol. 66, No. 4, July/August 1980
12. Brian McLaughlin, 'The Future of the Village', *The Village*, Vol. 31, No. 3, 1976
13. *The Decline of Rural Services* (Standing Conference of Rural Community Councils, 1978)
14. See, for example, Frank Dobson, 'Rural Health Services', *Medicine and Society*, Vol. 10, No. 3, autumn 1984; Peter Wedge, 'Out of Town: Rural Social Work, Questions to be Asked', *Community Care*, 22 November 1984; Stephen Woollett, *Alternative Rural Services* (NCVO, 1981); Rodney Willett, *Village Ventures* (Bedford Square Press/NCVO, 1985)

Chapter 11

1. Janet Hickman, *The King of the Barbareens* (Putnam, 1960)
2. in *The Times*, 7 September 1978
3. L.C. Comber et. al., *The Social Effects of Rural Primary School: Reorganisation, Final Report* (University of Aston, 1981)
4. Adrian Bell and Alan Sigsworth, *The Small Rural Primary School: A Matter of Quality* (Falmer Press, 1987)
5. Ibid. The authors cite Diana Forsythe (ed.), *The Rural Community and the Small School* (Aberdeen University Press, 1983) and R. Mordey and E. Judge, 'Rural service provisions and rural settlement policy', *Brunswick Environmental Papers*, No. 47 (Leeds Polytechnic, 1984)

6. Bell and Sigsworth provide an illustrative calculation of the costs involved in rural primary school reorganization.

7. Edmond Holmes, *What Is and What Might Be* (Constable, 1911)

8. Geoffrey Elsmore, reported in *The Times Educational Supplement*, 28 September 1984

9. Department of Education and Science, draft circular *Providing for Quality: The Pattern of Organisation to age 19*, August 1986, and *Better Schools*, Cmd 9469 (HMSO, 1985)

10. *The Times*, 6 May 1987

11. Department of Education and Science *Circular 3/87*, 8 May 1987

12. *The Conspiracy Against Village Schools*, published by Christopher Bunyan on behalf of Easton Royal School supporters, 1986, is obtainable from the National Association for the Support of Small Schools, 91 King Street, Norwich NR1 1PH

13. NASSS *Newsletter*, January 1987

14. Kenneth Baker on *Today*, BBC Radio 4, 7 May 1987

15. *The Conspiracy Against Village Schools*, op. cit.

16. Rural Music Schools Association, Little Benslow Hills, Hitchin, Herts SG4 9RB

17. Susannah Kirkman, 'Splendid isolation', *The Times Educational Supplement*, 1 May 1987

18. David Clark, *Small Schools: What are the Conditions and Factors Affecting Small Schools' Co-operation* (unpublished dissertation, School of Education, University of Exeter, 1986)

19. Bell and Sigsworth, op. cit.

20. Ibid.

21. Ibid., citing R. Gregory, 'The educational advantages of the small primary school', *Forum*, Vol. 17, No. 3, summer 1975

22. W.J. Campbell, 'School size: its influence on pupils' in A. Finch and P. Scrimshaw (eds.), *Standards, Schooling and Education* (Hodder & Stoughton, 1980)

23. Sarah Bayliss, 'Village schools survive by local funds say heads', *The Times Educational Supplement*, 21 March 1986

24. 'No to parents' offer of £7,500 DIY classroom', *East Anglian Daily Times*, 24 June 1981

25. *Evening News*, 7 January 1977

26. Paul Harrison, 'Self service: the village that refused to abolish its school meals', *The Times Educational Supplement*, 19 June 1987

Chapter 12

1. M.S. Patel, *The Educational Philosophy of Mahatma Gandhi* (Navajivan Publishing House, Ahmedabad, 1953)
2. Helena Norberg-Hodge in *Resurgence*, May/June 1985 (after spending ten years in Ladakh)
3. John Rae, *The Eton of Africa*, produced by Desmond Lapsley, BBC 1, 9 September 1987
4. David Mulwa, *Master and Servant* (Longman, Kenya, 1979; Longman's African Classics, 1986)
5. J. Synge, 'The Selective Function and British Rural Education', *British Journal of Educational Studies*, Vol. XXIII, No. 2, June 1975
6. Ibid.
7. Ibid.
8. Ibid. The author is citing a huge accumulation of evidence, including John Saville, *Rural Depopulation in England and Wales* (Routledge & Kegan Paul, 1957), N. Hans, 'Regional Provision for Post-Primary Education in England',*Yearbook of Education*, 1939, and E.W. Martin, *The Shearers and the Shorn* (Routledge & Kegan Paul, 1965)
9. Muriel Clegg, 'Private Enterprise in Education', *The Suffolk Review*, Vol. 5, No. 2, summer 1981
10. Arthur and Constance Williams, *This Land of England* (Channel 4 Publications, 1986)
11. NUT, *The Struggle for Education* (Schoolmaster Publishing, 1970)
12. Stephen Humphries, *Hooligans or Rebels? An Oral History of Working-Class Childhood and Youth 1889–1939* (Basil Blackwell, 1981). Philip W. Gardner, *The Lost Elementary Schools of Victorian England* (Croom Helm, 1974)
13. See, for example, Jean Russell-Gebbett, *Henslow of Hitcham* (Terence Dalton Ltd, 1977)
14. Ronald Blythe, foreword to Jon Wyand, *Village Schools: A Future for the Past?* (Evans Brothers, 1980)
15. Argyll Commission, *Elementary Schools, Second Report* 1867, cited by J. Synge, op. cit.
16. Elliot Wigginton (adviser), *The Foxfire Book*, 1–5 (Foxfire Fund Inc, Rabun Gap, Georgia 30568, USA, 1972–9)
17. The Earl of Portsmouth, *A Knot of Roots* (Geoffrey Bles, 1965)
18. Peter Newsam, 'The Fable of Fred', a recollection of Sir Alec Clegg, *The Times Educational Supplement*, 7 February 1986
19. John Burnett (ed.), *Destiny Obscure: Autobiographies of Childhood*,

Education and Family from the 1820s to the 1920s (Allen Lane, 1982)

20. Sylvia Bond (ed.), *Yesteryears – School, Work and Leisure* (Interprint, 1979)
21. A.C. Hilton and J.E. Audric, *The School Farm* (Harrap, 1945)

Chapter 13

1. Reg Groves, *Sharpen the Sickle: the History of the Farmworkers' Union* (Porcupine Press, 1949)
2. Bertram Edwards, *The Burston School Strike* (Lawrence & Wishart, 1974)
3. See Betka Zamyska, *The Burston Rebellion* (BBC Ariel Books, 1985) and T.G. Higdon, *The Burston Rebellion* (republished 1984 by Trustees of the Burston Strike School, Scole Common, Diss, Norfolk)
4. *The Times Educational Supplement*, 25 April 1986
5. Alun Howkins, *Poor Labouring Men: Rural Radicalism in Norfolk 1870–1923* (Routledge & Kegan Paul, 1975)
6. Emily Wilby, 'Our School Strike', quoted in Bertram Edwards, op. cit.
7. Henry Morris, *The Village College: Being a Memorandum on the Provision of Educational and Social Facilities for the Countryside* (Cambridge University Press, 1924), reprinted in Harry Rée (ed.), *The Henry Morris Collection* (Cambridge University Press, 1984) and in Harry Rée, *Educator Extraordinary. The Life and Achievement of Henry Morris 1889–1961* (Peter Owen, 1985)
8. Ibid.
9. Harry Rée, 'A Case of Arrested Development?', *The Times Educational Supplement*, 17 October 1980
10. Philip Toogood, *The Head's Tale* (Dialogue Publications, 1984)
11. Jon Wyand, *Village Schools: A Future for the Past?* (Evans, 1980)
12. Richard Boston in *The Guardian*, 28 August 1984
13. Colin Hodgetts, 'Reflections on The Small School of Hartland', *Resurgence*, September/October 1986

Chapter 14

1. Walter T. Martin, 'Ecological change in satellite rural areas', *American Sociological Review*, April 1957
2. Peter Hall, 'Flight to the green', *New Society*, 9 January 1987

3. James D. Tarver, 'Gradients of Urban Influence on the Educational, Employment, and Fertility Patterns of Women', *Rural Sociology*, September 1969
4. Hedrick Smith, *The Russians* (Sphere Books, 1976)
5. Peter Lloyd, *Slums of Hope? Shanty towns of the third world* (Penguin Books, 1979)
6. World Health Organization, *Report of World Health*, 1984
7. David Morley and Hermione Lovel, *My Name is Today: child health, society and poverty in less developed countries* (Macmillan, 1986)
8. See M. Lipton, *Why Poor People Stay Poor: a study of urban bias in world development* (Temple Smith, 1977) and R. Chambers, *Rural Development: putting the last first* (Longmans, 1983)
9. Jon Bennett, with Susan George, *The Hunger Machine* (Polity Press, 1987)
10. Morley and Lovel, op. cit.
11. José Arthur Rios, quoted in Peter Wilsher and Rosemary Righter *The Exploding Cities* (André Deutsch, 1975)
12. Bryan Roberts, *Cities of Peasants* (Edward Arnold, 1978)
13. Jon Bennett, op. cit.
14. Kevin Lynch, *Growing Up in Cities*, Studies of the Spatial Environment of Adolescence in Cracow, Melbourne, Mexico City, Salta, Toluca and Warsaw (MIT Press, 1978)

Chapter 15

1. In C. Delisle Burns, *Leisure in the Modern World* (Allen & Unwin, 1932)
2. Theodore Dreiser, *Dawn*, 1931, quoted by Morton and Lucia White, *The Intellectual Versus the City* (Mentor Books, 1962)
3. Susan Hale, *The Idle Hill: a prospect for young workers in a rural area* (Bedford Square Press, 1971)
4. Stanley Cohen, 'Property Destruction: motives and meanings' in C. Ward (ed.), *Vandalism* (Architectural Press, 1973)
5. Allan Kennedy, *Shadows of Adolescence* (National Youth Bureau, 1984)
6. Susan Hale, op. cit.
7. Allan Kennedy, op. cit.
8. Frances Reynolds, *The Problem Housing Estate* (Gower, 1986)
9. Allan Kennedy, op. cit.
10. Simon Nicholson, *Out of Town, Out of Mind? A Study of Rural*

Unemployment (Leicester Diocesan Board for Social Responsibility, 1986)
11. Susan Hale, op. cit.
12. Allan Kennedy, op. cit.
13. J.E. Bessell, *The Younger Worker in Agriculture* (National Economic Development Office, 1976)

Chapter 16

1. Colin Ward, *The Child in the City* (Architectural Press, 1978)
2. Mary Chamberlain, *Fenwomen: A Portrait of Women in an English Village* (Virago, 1975)
3. Eddie Double, 'Can the Village School Survive?', paper given at the seminar held by the Centre for the Study of Rural Society, Lincoln, 1978
4. Roy Whittaker and Alan Sigsworth, 'Rural Isolation: a cautionary research comment' in *Educational Disadvantage in Rural Areas* (Centre for Information and Advice on Rural Disadvantage, 1980)
5. Ibid.
6. 'Living in poverty next to affluence', interview with Brian McLaughlin in *Rural Viewpoint*, Issue 14, September 1985
7. Simon Nicholson, *Out of Town Out of Mind?: a Study of rural unemployment* (Leicester Diocesan Board for Social Responsibility, 1985)
8. Malcolm Moseley, *Rural Development and its Relevance to the Inner City Debate* (Social Science Research Council, 1980)
9. Vilhelm Aubert, 'Rural Poverty and Community Isolation' in Peter Townsend (ed.), *The Concept of Poverty* (Heinemann, 1970)
10. 'The One-Room Schoolhouse', *Manas* (Los Angeles), 2 October 1985
11. Susan Hale, *The Idle Hill: a prospect for young workers in a rural area* (Bedford Square Press, 1971)
12. Simon Nicholson, op. cit.
13. M.J. Moseley, 'Rural Mobility and Accessibility' in J.M. Shaw (ed.), *Rural Deprivation and Planning*, (Geo Books, 1982)
14. Malcolm J. Moseley, 'Is Rural Deprivation Really Rural?', *The Planner* Vol. 66, No. 4, July/August 1980
15. See 'The Rural-Urban Continuum Debate' in T.G. McGee, *The Urbanization Process in the Third World* (G. Bell & Son, 1971)

Chapter 17

1. Cited by W.G. Hoskins and L. Dudley Stamp in *The Common Lands of England and Wales* (Collins, 1963)
2. John Barrell, 'The Golden Age of Labour' in Mabey, Clifford and King (eds.), *Second Nature* (Jonathan Cape, 1984)
3. Ebenezer Howard at the London School of Economics, 18 July 1904
4. Anthony King, *The Bungalow: The production of a Global Culture* (Routledge & Kegan Paul, 1984)
5. Dennis Hardy and Colin Ward, *Arcadia for All: The Legacy of a Makeshift Culture* (Mansell, 1984)
6. *Directions for Change: Land Use in the 1990s* (National Economic Development Council, 1987)
7. Robin Grove-White, addressing the Annual General Meeting of the Open Spaces Society, 8 July 1987
8. *Comments on Department of the Environment Draft Circular* 'Development Involving Agricultural Land' (Town and Country Planning Association, 10 April 1987)
9. Roy Gazzard, at the 'People and Planning' Conference, Newcastle Polytechnic, 21 October 1972, *Newcastle Journal*, 23 October 1972
10. Peter Hall (ed.), *The Inner City in Context*, Final Report of the SSRC Inner Cities Working Party (Heinemann, 1981)
11. Maurice Ash, *New Renaissance* (Green Books, 1987)
12. Professor Lewis Keeple in *The Planner*, June 1986, discussing Martin J. Elson, *Green Belts: Conflict Mediation in the Urban Fringe* (Heinemann, 1986)
13. Shankland, Willmott and Jordan, *Inner London, Policies for Dispersal and Balance* (HMSO, 1977)
14. Michael Salt, letter to *The Guardian*, 8 June 1986
15. *Diverse Report*, Channel 4, 11 June 1986, kindly reported to me by Tim Mars
16. Peter Hall, 'Flight to the green', *New Society*, 9 January 1987 (summarizing current research by Paul Cheshire, Denis Hay and Peter Hall)
17. *Rural Resettlement Handbook*, third edition (Prism Publications, Sherborne, Dorset, 1984)
18. Robert Van de Weyer, *Wickwyn: A Vision of the Future* (SPCK, 1986)
19. Robert Van de Weyer, 'Unwalled Village', *Resurgence*, May–June 1987
20. 'About Anglia', Anglia TV, November 1986

21. Colin Ward, *When We Build Again, Let's have housing that works* (Pluto Press, 1985)

Further Reading

At first sight it seems simple to provide a list of further reading about the child in the country. The problem is one of where to stop. My own sources, familiar or recondite, are listed in the notes.

But what readily accessible books should be recommended to the reader who wants to pursue the theme further? The difficulty is that while many a bookshop has a section for 'country books', few of the volumes it contains, apart from the valuable accumulation of personal life histories, attempt to put rural childhood in a historical and social setting. Truths about the country child are less in demand than popular mythology or the cult of nostalgia. Even in libraries it isn't easy to find the right shelf. Are we looking for history, sociology, education or local studies? There are, all the same, a number of outstanding authors and excellent books.

The history of country childhood in England and Wales from Victorian times to the First World War is told in a whole series of books by Pamela Horn. They are *The Victorian Country Child* (Roundswood Press, 1974; new edition Alan Sutton, 1985), *Education in Rural England 1800–1914* (Gill & Macmillan, 1978), *The Rural World 1790–1850: Social Change in the English Countryside* (Hutchinson, 1980), *The Changing Countryside in Victorian and Edwardian England and Wales* (Athlone Press, 1984), and *Rural Life in England in the First World War* (Gill & Macmillan, 1984).

FURTHER READING

The new interest in oral history has led to a variety of books including childhood recollections epitomised in Paul Thompson's *The Edwardians* (Weidenfeld & Nicolson, 1975; Paladin, 1977) and Thea Thompson's *Edwardian Childhoods* (Routledge & Kegan Paul, 1981). A guide to this whole field is provided by Paul Thompson's *The Voice of the Past* (Oxford University Press, 1978) and by magazines like *History Workshop Journal* (Routledge & Kegan Paul) and *Oral History* (Dept of Sociology, University of Essex).

The best recent accounts of contemporary rural life are Howard Newby's *Country Life: A Social History of Rural England* (Weidenfeld & Nicolson, 1987) and Anthony Russell's *The Country Parish* (SPCK, 1986). By far the most important book on rural education is Adrian Bell and Alan Sigsworth's *The Small Rural Primary School: A Matter of Quality* (Falmer Press, 1987).

Index

INDEX